PRAIRIE CHILDREN
& THEIR QUILTS

W9-BRM-774

KATHLEEN TRACY

PRAIRIE CHILDREN

Martingale®
& COMPANY

Their Quilts

14 Little Projects That Honor the Pioneer Spirit

Prairie Children and Their Quilts: 14 Little Projects That Honor the Pioneer Spirit
© 2006 by Kathleen Tracy

That Patchwork Place® is an imprint of Martingale & Company®.

Martingale & Company
20205 144th Avenue NE
Woodinville, WA 98072-8478 USA
www.martingale-pub.com

CREDITS

President: *Nancy J. Martin*
CEO: *Daniel J. Martin*
COO: *Tom Wierzbicki*
Publisher: *Jane Hamada*
Editorial Director: *Mary V. Green*
Managing Editor: *Tina Cook*
Technical Editor: *Ellen Pahl*
Copy Editor: *Melissa Bryan*
Design Director: *Stan Green*
Illustrator: *Laurel Strand*
Cover Designer: *Stan Green*
Text Designer: *Trina Craig*
Photographer: *Brent Kane*

MISSION STATEMENT

Dedicated to providing quality products
and service to inspire creativity.

No part of this product may be reproduced in any form, unless otherwise stated, in which case reproduction is limited to the use of the purchaser. The written instructions, photographs, designs, projects, and patterns are intended for the personal, noncommercial use of the retail purchaser and are under federal copyright laws; they are not to be reproduced by any electronic, mechanical, or other means, including informational storage or retrieval systems, for commercial use. Permission is granted to photocopy patterns for the personal use of the retail purchaser.

The information in this book is presented in good faith, but no warranty is given nor results guaranteed. Since Martingale & Company has no control over choice of materials or procedures, the company assumes no responsibility for the use of this information.

Printed in China
11 10 09 08 07 06   8 7 6 5 4 3 2 1

Library of Congress Cataloging-in-Publication Data
Library of Congress Control Number: 2006014363

ISBN-13: 978-1-56477-686-0
ISBN-10: 1-56477-686-7

Diary entries on pages 11, 12, 20, 21, 29, 30, 35, 42, and 60 reprinted from *Covered Wagon Women,* edited and compiled by Kenneth L. Holmes by permission of the University of Nebraska Press. Copyright by Kenneth L. Holmes. Reprinted by the University of Nebraska Press by arrangement with the Arthur H. Clark Company.

PHOTO CREDITS

The sources for the photographs in this book are listed below:

Contents page and page 11, *Wagon Train,* X-21874; contents page and page 20, *Pioneer Family,* X-11929, courtesy of the Denver Public Library, Western History Collection.

Contents page and page 29, *A Funeral in Pioneer Days;* contents page and page 35, *Pioneers by Their Log Cabin;* page 50, *Building for the Future;* page 60, *Rural School,* from the Fred Hultstrand History in Pictures Collection, NDIRS-NDSU, Fargo, North Dakota

Contents page and page 42, *Indian Girls and Tipis,* LC USZ62-120768, courtesy of the Library of Congress

Book cover, dedication page, page 9, and page 10, *Pioneer Girl and Her Doll;* page 78, *Early Transportation in the Dakotas,* courtesy of Diana Brown, Outwest Photographs

Title pages and page 8, from author's private collection

Dedication

For Paul, with love; and for Evan and Caitlin, my greatest inspiration

Acknowledgments

Special thanks to the staff at Martingale, especially Terry Martin, Karen Soltys, Mary Green, and Tina Cook, for their enthusiasm, encouragement, and support of this project.

Thanks to Ellen Pahl and Melissa Bryan for their editorial expertise.

Thanks to Victor Brandt for the generous loan of his dolls shown on the cover and in the photos on pages 10 and 40. The dolls were made from kits designed and produced by Gail Wilson.

Thanks to Jane Graff for inspiring "Little Red Schoolhouse Quilt" on page 62.

Thanks to Elaine Maruhn at the University of Nebraska Press for granting permission to reprint excerpts from *Covered Wagon Women,* vols. I, V, and VIII, edited and compiled by Kenneth L. Holmes.

Thanks especially to Ingrid, Linda, and Julia for their friendship and support throughout the writing of this book.

Finally, thanks to my family for their love and encouragement.

CONTENTS

Preface

As a young girl, history classes were my least favorite because they seemed to focus on men and their accomplishments or wars and massacres, interspersed with dates that needed to be memorized. There were few women in history textbooks to whom young girls could relate. It wasn't until my children began school and encountered wonderful, creative teachers that I relearned (and relived) American history along with them. Textbooks and resources used by teachers today particularly take note of the fact that women played a huge part in the development of America and that ordinary women of the past can be important role models for girls today.

My interest in and curiosity about antique quilts led me to try to find out more about their origins and the lives of the women who made them. Children aren't the only ones who learn best while they're having fun! I hope that, like me, you find a renewed pride in our country's heritage through the making of these simple little prairie quilts and see just what a significant role quilting played in the lives of the women and children we call the pioneers.

INTRODUCTION

Come my tan-faced children,
Follow well in order, get your weapons ready,
Have you your pistols? have you your sharp-
    edged axes?
Pioneers! O pioneers!

For we cannot tarry here,
We must march my darlings, we must bear the
    brunt of danger,
We the youthful sinewy races, all the rest on
    us depend,
Pioneers! O pioneers!
. . . .
O you daughters of the West!
O you young and elder daughters! O you
    mothers and you wives!
Never must you be divided, in our ranks you
    move united,
Pioneers! O pioneers!
    —Walt Whitman, "Pioneers! O Pioneers!"
        from *Leaves of Grass*

WHAT WOULD LIFE have been like for children growing up in the nineteenth century on the American frontier? It was certainly a period of change for the country as crowded eastern cities and opportunities to own good farming land encouraged westward expansion. History books have given us numerous accounts of the struggles of the courageous men who settled the West, but what role did women and children play in that endeavor? Many women took along diaries to record their travels and express their personal feelings about the journey. We are fortunate to have those accounts available for clues about their daily lives. Journal accounts written by children are rare, but some do exist. It's likely that children had a much different experience than the adults. Many of the diary excerpts reveal an excitement and anticipation of the adventures they were about to embark upon, coupled with realistic narratives of the harsh realities and sorrows encountered on the trail.

While life on the prairie involved much hard work for even the youngest children, this must have been a great adventure, and diaries may have been kept so that the experiences could be remembered and passed down through families, in much the same way that quilts were used as legacies of the past.

If the pioneer era was an important stage in American history, it was equally as important in the history of American quilting. More quilts were made during this period than ever before, due in part to the rapidly expanding textile industry and the wide availability of inexpensive fabric, but also due to an increased demand as quilts were needed for the westward journey and the many new settlements. Many of the traditional quilt-block patterns that we're familiar with today were named or renamed after the pioneers' daily experiences. These blocks tell the story of the settling of the western territories through the pieces of calico and other fabric scraps that were stitched into quilts.

Examples of doll quilts from this period are rare. The quilts and patterns included in this book are not based on actual antique doll quilts from the time but merely draw inspiration from the adventures the pioneers faced and the hardships they endured as the West was settled. While we do not know for sure what kinds of quilts the children might have made, we do know which styles were popular during the pioneer period. Looking at the photos from the past and reading the diaries, we can see how the events of frontier life must have shaped the designs of the quilts that were made in this era. It was during this time in America that women's lives were truly pieced in the quilts.

The chapters that follow will take you on a journey through the pioneers' chapter in American history—the reasons many had for making the trip, the ups and downs of daily life on the trail, the courage the settlers showed when faced with trouble, and the building of their new homes and schools. You'll read actual words written by children who made the trek and see photos of the way they lived. Patterns for 14 simple little quilts and projects reflecting life on the prairie complete *your* journey.

Few of the children became famous; their names are not mentioned in history books. They were not traditional heroes, these children, but their very existence should be considered heroic. How ordinary their lives were, and yet how extraordinary they became in the face of the challenges that were presented to them on a daily basis. Diaries and photos will never tell us all we want to know about these children's lives, but we can give value to those lives and meaning to their existence by celebrating their adventurous spirits. As we read their words, the tales enhance our lives and we gain a true perspective of the enduring strength of the pioneer spirit.

Leaving Home

"The last good bye has been said — the last glimpse of our old home on the hill, and wave of hand at the old Academy, with a good bye to kind teachers and schoolmates, and we are off."

—Sallie Hester, age 14, 1849

The MID-NINETEENTH CENTURY was a time of dramatic growth in America. Tempted by stories of lush farmland that was generally considered free for the taking with few government restrictions, thousands of settlers headed west. Eager to homestead and hopeful about the possibility of financial success, they heeded the call of the open lands. Many had never traveled more than a few miles from home. The reasons for flocking westward were varied. Farmers from the eastern states, disillusioned with urban culture, overcrowding, and poor farmland, first moved to places like Missouri and the Midwest, and then eventually were lured by the wide-open spaces of Oregon, Washington, and California. Some were Swedish, German, and Norwegian immigrants who had come to America desiring better lives as well as the opportunity to own their own land. Some, like the Mormons, fled religious intolerance in their own country. Freed black slaves also wished to escape the prejudicial attitudes of the South and sought freedom to pursue their dreams. All wanted better lives and headed westward with great hopes of what the future could bring.

The men were the ones who were struck by "Oregon fever," and while they followed their ambitions and the seemingly unlimited opportunities for prosperity in the West, the women often had no other choice but to follow their husbands.

Numerous preparations had to be made in advance of the trip, sometimes taking months of planning. Houses, farms, and many possessions were sold, for only the most important items that would fit into the wagons, or prairie schooners, were allowed.

To leave behind the familiarity and safety of home must have been the most difficult thing of all. At age 14, Sallie Hester wrote: "Our train numbered fifty wagons. The last hours were spent in bidding goodbye to old friends. My mother is heartbroken over this separation of relatives and friends."

Two of the most common items that young girls brought with them on their journey were dolls and diaries. Dolls were among a young girl's most cherished possessions and were probably chosen for the comfort they provided in the face of uncertain circumstances and the sadness of leaving behind friends, relatives, and homes.

The women brought quilts that were made and given by friends and relatives. They were special reminders of friendship, many containing signatures or special pieces of fabric from the clothing of the maker as personal touches. With excitement and sadness combined, quilters sometimes put months of work and their best efforts into making beautiful quilts that were destined to be given away and treasured as heirlooms. Friendship quilts may also have helped ease the anxieties of the travelers about what lay ahead and the all-too-evident awareness that the paths of beloved friends and relatives might never cross again. What poignant and delightful reminders of lives left behind these quilts must have been!

Yet while the adventurous aspect of the trip might have been the exciting part for the children, most children were probably unaware of and unprepared for the dangers and uncertainties they would face as their long journey began.

FRIENDSHIP STAR QUILT

The Friendship Star block is one that was filled with sentiment. When pioneer families headed west, friends and relatives would send quilts with them to commemorate special relationships. These quilts were sometimes treated as heirlooms and stored in trunks, and only when the settlers arrived at their destination would they unpack the quilts to remind them of the loving hands that made them back home.

Materials

Yardages are based on 42"-wide, 100%-cotton fabrics.

✦ ⅛ yard *each* of 12 different light prints for star backgrounds

✦ ⅛ yard *each* of 12 different medium prints for star points

✦ ⅓ yard of blue floral print for outer border

✦ ¼ yard of pink print for inner border

✦ Scraps of 12 different medium prints for star centers

✦ ¼ yard of brown print for binding

✦ ¾ yard of fabric for backing

✦ 24" x 28" piece of cotton batting

Cutting

From *each* of the 12 light prints, cut:

✦ 2 squares, 2⅜" x 2⅜" (24 squares total)

✦ 4 squares, 2" x 2" (48 squares total)

From *each* of the 12 medium prints for star points, cut:

✦ 2 squares, 2⅜" x 2⅜" (24 squares total)

From *each* of the 12 medium prints for star centers, cut:

✦ 1 square, 2" x 2" (12 squares total)

From the pink print, cut:

✦ 2 strips, 1¼" x 42"; crosscut into 2 pieces, 1¼" x 15½", and 2 pieces, 1¼" x 18½"

From the blue floral print, cut:

✦ 2 strips, 3" x 42"; crosscut into 2 pieces, 3" x 20", and 2 pieces, 3" x 20½"

From the brown print, cut:

✦ 3 strips, 1½" x 42"

Assembly

It's easiest to make this quilt one block at a time, selecting four 2" squares and two 2⅜" squares from the same light print, and two 2⅜" squares from the same medium print. That way, the star points and the background will be consistent within each block.

1. Draw a diagonal line from corner to corner on the wrong side of each 2⅜" light print square. Layer each marked square on top of a 2⅜" medium print square, right sides together. Stitch ¼" from the line on both sides, and cut on the drawn line. Press the seams toward the darker fabric. Make a total of 48 half-square-triangle units.

Make 48 in matching sets of 4.

2. Sew four matching units from step 1, four matching 2" light print squares, and a 2" square of a contrasting medium print together as shown to make a Friendship Star block. Press the seams as shown. Repeat to make 12 blocks.

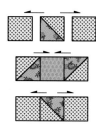

Make 12.

3. Sew the blocks together into four rows of three blocks each. Press the seams in the opposite direction from row to row. Sew the rows together, and press the seams in one direction.

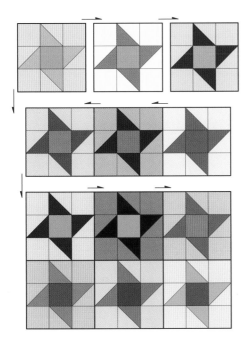

4. Sew the 1¼" x 18½" pink strips to the sides of the quilt top, pressing the seam allowances toward the border. Sew the 1¼" x 15½" pink strips to the top and bottom of the quilt top and press.

5. Sew the 3" x 20" blue floral strips to the sides of the quilt top, pressing the seam allowances toward the outer border. Sew the 3" x 20½" blue floral strips to the top and bottom of the quilt top and press.

Quilt Finishing

1. Layer the quilt top, batting, and backing, and baste the layers together as shown in "Putting the Quilt Together" on page 75.

2. Quilt an X through the center of each block.

3. Attach the brown print binding to the quilt, referring to "Single-Fold Binding" on page 76.

Signature Quilt

Quilts from cherished friends and relatives back home were reminders of the comfortable lives and people left behind. The sentiments inscribed on these quilts and the memories they embodied surely helped western travelers cope with loneliness and make the transition to their new lives.

Materials

Yardages are based on 42"-wide, 100%-cotton fabrics.

- ⅛ yard *each* or scraps of 6 assorted medium prints for blocks
- ¼ yard of light blue floral print for inner border
- ¼ yard of beige floral print for outer border
- ⅛ yard of muslin for blocks
- Scraps of 12 assorted medium prints for blocks
- ¼ yard of green print for binding
- ⅝ yard of fabric for backing
- 20" x 25" piece of cotton batting
- Freezer paper
- Fine-point permanent fabric pen in black or brown (such as Pigma .001)
- 1⅝ yards of ⅛"-wide maroon satin ribbon for embellishing

Cutting

From *each* of 6 assorted medium prints, cut:
- 2 squares, 2½" x 2½" (12 squares total)
- 1 square, 2⅞" x 2⅞" (6 squares total); cut each square in half diagonally once (12 triangles total)

From the muslin, cut:
- 6 rectangles, 2½" x 4½"

From *each* of 12 assorted medium-print scraps, cut:
- 1 square, 2⅞" x 2⅞" (12 squares total); cut each square in half diagonally once (24 triangles total; you will use 1 of each print)

From the light blue floral print, cut:
- 2 strips, 1¾" x 42"; crosscut into 2 pieces, 1¾" x 11", and 2 pieces, 1¾" x 12½"

From the beige floral print, cut:
- 2 strips, 3" x 42"; crosscut into 2 pieces, 3" x 15", and 2 pieces, 3" x 16"

From the green print, cut:
- 3 strips, 1½" x 42"

Assembly

1. Draw a diagonal line from corner to corner on the wrong side of each 2½" medium print square.

2. Layer a marked square on one end of a 2½" x 4½" muslin rectangle, right sides together, as shown. Sew on the line and trim to a ¼" seam allowance. Press the triangle toward the corner. Place a matching marked square on the other end of the rectangle, right sides together, making sure the diagonal line is oriented in the opposite direction from the first piece. Stitch on the drawn line. Trim to a ¼" seam allowance and press the triangle toward the corner. Make a total of six flying-geese units.

Make 6.

3. Lay out the pieces for each block in advance, using the flying-geese units and the triangles cut from 2⅞" squares of medium prints. Pair the triangles that match the prints on the flying-geese units

with the triangles cut from scraps, right sides together. Stitch along the diagonal using a ¼" seam allowance. Press the seams toward the darker fabric.

Make 12.

4. Sew the triangle squares together and press toward the darker fabric. Join each of these units with a matching flying-geese unit to make the signature blocks. Press the seams after arranging the blocks so that they will butt together.

Make 6.

5. Sew the blocks together into three rows of two blocks each, pressing the seams in the opposite direction from row to row.

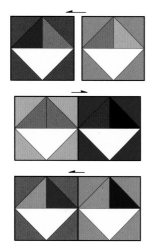

6. Sew the 1¾" x 11" blue floral strips to the sides of the quilt top, pressing the seam allowances toward the border. Sew the 1¾" x 12½" blue floral strips to the top and bottom of the quilt top and press.

7. Sew the 3" x 15" beige floral strips to the sides of the quilt top, pressing the seams toward the outer border. Sew the 3" x 16" beige floral strips to the top and bottom of the quilt top and press.

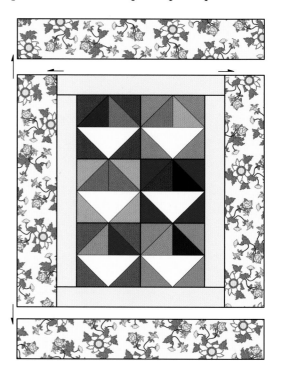

8. Cut four 4" x 4" squares of freezer paper and cut twice diagonally. Iron a triangle of freezer paper onto the back of each muslin triangle to stabilize it for writing. Using the fine-point permanent fabric marker, add signatures or lines from a favorite quote on the muslin triangles. Remove the freezer paper carefully. Layer a small piece of muslin over the block and press with a dry iron to set the ink.

Finishing the Quilt

1. Layer the quilt top, batting, and backing, and baste the layers together as shown in "Putting the Quilt Together" on page 75.

2. Quilt in the ditch around each triangle and each block.

3. Attach the green print binding to the quilt, referring to "Single-Fold Binding" on page 76.

4. Hand stitch the maroon satin ribbon along the seam line between the inner and outer borders.

Children today are rarely taught domestic skills from the past. Yet even in our present hurried world, learning practical sewing skills can give young people a great sense of satisfaction in mastering a craft. As children gain confidence in their creative abilities, they experience the ultimate joy of artistic expression. Making doll quilts is one craft children can absolutely accomplish successfully and progress to more difficult projects with practice.

LIFE ON THE TRAIL

"Only think of not sleeping in a bed for 6 or 7 months not eating at a table drinking out of tin cups eating on tin plates spread on the ground."

—Louisa Cook, 1862

THE WAGONS LEFT in the spring, when the grass had turned green for the cattle to graze on and to ensure, hopefully, that the travelers would arrive at their destination before the first winter snows. Families traveled in groups for safety and companionship along the way. Often, hundreds of wagons could be seen crawling slowly across the plains. Sallie Hester, 14 years old in 1849, recalled in her diary of the journey, "As far as eye can reach, so great is the emigration, you see nothing but wagons."

The average journey took four or five months and was, by most accounts, a grueling trip. Riding in the wagons was not particularly comfortable and many travelers made the trip partly on foot, carrying children when the road proved too rugged and the wagon too bumpy. Boys as young as 10 walked alongside the wagons, driving the cattle. The comfortable lives left behind faded into memory as hardships became a part of the daily struggle to survive and reach the journey's end.

On the trail, families still had to perform daily chores, although in a much more difficult way, hampered by primitive conditions. Some of the older children gave details of trail life in their diaries. In 1849, Sallie Hester wrote: "We have a cooking stove made of sheet iron, a portable table, tin plates and cups, cheap knives and forks (best ones packed away), camp stools, etc. . . . We live on bacon, ham, rice, dried fruits, molasses, packed butter, bread, coffee, tea and milk as we have our own cows."

Sleeping outdoors was customary when the weather permitted, but fear of attack by Indians or wild animals left the families with a measure of insecurity and they often slept crowded together in the wagons or in tents pitched for the night. Sallie Hester recounted the experience: "When we camp at night we form a corral with our wagons and pitch our tents on the outside, and inside of this corral we drive our cattle, with guards stationed on the outside of the tents. . . . We sleep in our wagons on feather beds; the men who drive for us in the tents."

Dolls played an important role in the lives of the girls who made the trip across the plains. Since children were allowed to bring along few playthings, the favored doll was often the choice. In looking at photos from the time period, we are struck by the number of girls who posed with their dolls. Clearly, dolls were more than playthings—they were cherished companions, too. The quilts made for the dolls may have been similarly treasured as well, although few original quilts exist today because of the extreme wear and tear they endured.

Women and children must have yearned for their old, familiar homes and comfortable surroundings. Many kept diaries and, to relieve the loneliness, spent time writing letters to friends and family back home. Tired and lonely, many women must have wondered why they had agreed to the journey in the first place. What a difficult endeavor it must have been! For others, the excitement at the thought of homesteading and starting new lives may have been a cause for optimism about the bright futures ahead.

Many westward travelers must have been awestruck by the beauty and wildness of those parts of the country they had never seen before. The prairies were lovely—who wouldn't have been entranced by the beauty of the wilderness and the wide-open spaces? Yet, on a daily basis, the pioneers faced struggles with Mother Nature that they had never imagined. Frontier families were survivors in the strongest sense of the word, doing what they needed to do to stay alive and reach their destinations safely.

BROKEN DISHES QUILT

The Broken Dishes pattern was one of the most popular designs of the time, and it tells us just how rugged the journey must have been. Roads were often bumpy, and breakable items such as dishes and glassware were wrapped in quilts to safeguard them. The wagons were so uncomfortable to ride in that many women and older children walked part of the way, carrying younger children and babies in their arms.

Materials

Yardages are based on 42"-wide, 100%-cotton fabrics.

- ⅛ yard *each* or scraps of 8 to 10 assorted blue, pink, and light prints for blocks
- ¼ yard of red check for outer border
- ⅛ yard of medium blue print for inner border
- Scraps of 2 red prints for blocks
- ¼ yard of dark blue print for binding
- ⅔ yard of fabric for backing
- 21" x 25" piece of cotton batting

Cutting

From the assorted light prints, cut:
- 15 squares, 2⅞" x 2⅞"

From the assorted pink prints, cut:
- 9 squares, 2⅞" x 2⅞"

From the assorted blue prints, cut:
- 20 squares, 2⅞" x 2⅞"

From the red scraps, cut:
- 4 squares, 2⅞" x 2⅞"

From the medium blue print for inner border, cut:
- 2 strips, 1¼" x 42"; crosscut into 2 pieces, 1¼" x 12½", and 2 pieces, 1¼" x 18"

From the red check, cut:
- 2 strips, 2½" x 42"; crosscut into 4 pieces, 2½" x 18"

From the dark blue print, cut:
- 3 strips, 1½" x 42"

Assembly

1. Draw a diagonal line from corner to corner on the wrong side of each 2⅞" light print and pink print square. At random, layer a marked square on top of a 2⅞" square of blue or red print, right sides together. Stitch ¼" from the line on both sides, and cut on the drawn line. Press the seams toward the darker fabric. Make 48.

Make 48.

2. Arrange four half-square-triangle units into a block, balancing color and value; use at least two matching units, or two that are very similar, in each block. Sew the units together as shown and press the seams. Repeat to make 12 Broken Dishes blocks.

Make 12.

3. Sew the blocks together into four rows of three blocks each. Press the seams in the opposite direction from row to row. Sew the rows together, and press the seams in one direction.

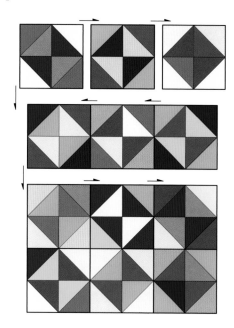

4. Sew the 1¼" x 12½" blue border strips to the top and bottom of the quilt top, pressing the seam allowances toward the border. Sew the 1¼" x 18" blue border strips to the sides of the quilt top and press.

5. Sew two of the 2½" x 18" red-checked strips to the sides of the quilt top, pressing the seam allowances toward the outer border. Sew the two remaining 2½" x 18" red-checked strips to the top and bottom of the quilt top and press.

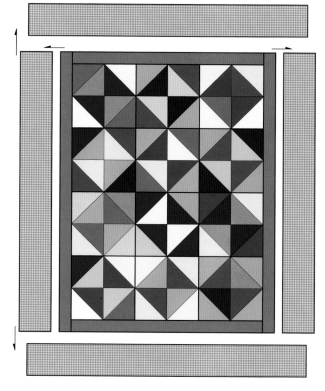

Finishing the Quilt

1. Layer the quilt top, batting, and backing, and baste the layers together as shown in "Putting the Quilt Together" on page 75.

2. Quilt in the ditch around each triangle and block.

3. Attach the dark blue print binding to the quilt, referring to "Single-Fold Binding" on page 76.

BEAR'S PAW QUILT

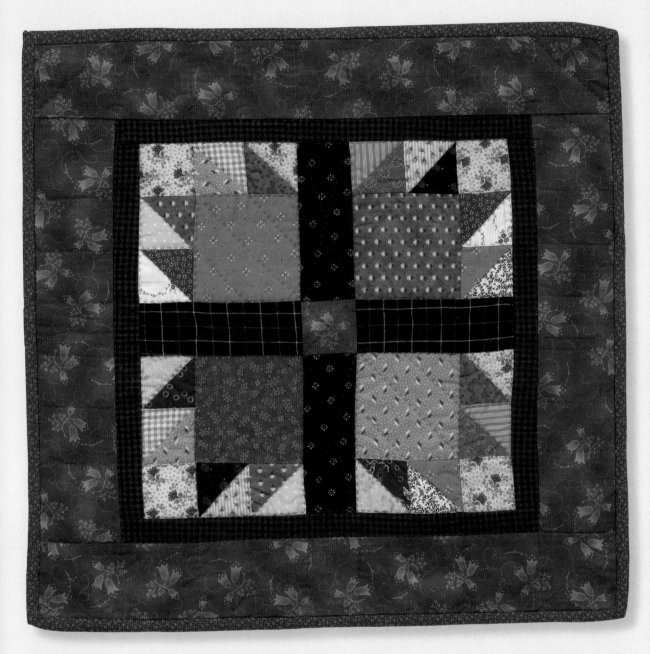

In the 1800s, the trail west was fraught with danger from many sources, including wildlife. Rattlesnakes, coyotes, wolves, and grizzly bears all roamed the Great Plains and posed a real threat to these early western travelers. ✒

Materials

Yardages are based on 42"-wide, 100%-cotton fabrics.

- ⅛ yard *each* or scraps of 6 to 12 medium prints for block
- ¼ yard of brown print for block center and outer border
- ⅛ yard *each* of 2 different black prints for block
- ⅛ yard of blue check for inner border
- Scraps of 6 to 12 light prints for block
- ¼ yard of maroon print for binding
- ¾ yard of fabric for backing
- 23" x 23" piece of cotton batting

Cutting

From the light prints, cut:
- 8 squares, 2⅝" x 2⅝"
- 4 matching squares, 2¼" x 2¼"

From *each* of 4 medium prints, cut:
- 1 square, 4" x 4" (4 squares total)

From the remaining scraps of medium prints, cut:
- 8 squares, 2⅝" x 2⅝"

From *each* of the 2 black prints, cut:
- 1 strip, 2¼" x 12" (2 strips total); crosscut into 2 pieces, 2¼" x 5¾" (4 pieces total)

From the brown print, cut:
- 1 square, 2¼" x 2¼"
- 2 strips, 3" x 42"; crosscut into 2 pieces, 3" x 14¼", and 2 pieces, 3" x 19¼"

From the blue check, cut:
- 2 strips, 1¼" x 40"; crosscut into 2 pieces, 1¼" x 12¾", and 2 pieces, 1¼" x 14¼"

From the maroon print, cut:
- 3 strips, 1½" x 42"

Assembly

1. Draw a diagonal line from corner to corner on the wrong side of each 2⅝" light print square. Layer a marked square on top of a 2⅝" medium square, right sides together. Stitch ¼" from the line on both sides, and cut on the drawn line. Press the seams toward the darker fabric. Make 16 half-square-triangle units.

Make 16.

2. Sew the half-square-triangle units together in pairs as shown. Press. Make four of each.

Make 4.　　　　Make 4.

3. Sew one of the units from step 2 to the top of a 4" medium print square, pressing the seams as shown. Make four.

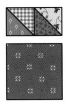

Make 4.

4. Sew a 2¼" light print square to each of the remaining units from step 2 as shown. Press toward the light print square.

Make 4.

5. Sew a unit from step 4 to one side of a unit from step 3 as shown. Press. Make four.

  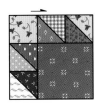

Make 4.

6. Sew pairs of paw units from step 5 together with two matching 2¼" x 5¾" black pieces as shown. Press the seams toward the black print. Sew the two remaining black pieces to opposite sides of the 2¼" brown print square. Press toward the black print.

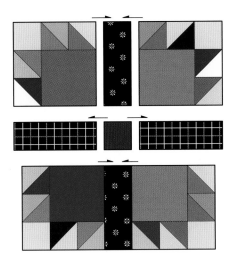

7. Sew the rows together to make the Bear's Paw block. Press.

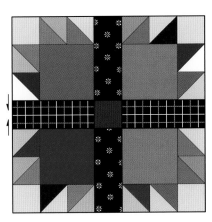

8. Sew the 1¼" x 12¾" blue-checked strips to the sides of the quilt top, pressing the seam allowances toward the border. Sew the 1¼" x 14¼" blue-checked strips to the top and bottom of the quilt top and press.

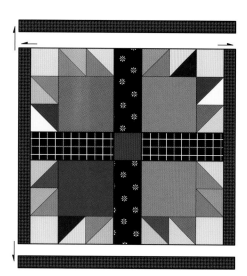

9. Sew the 3" x 14¼" brown print strips to the sides of the quilt top, pressing the seam allowances toward the outer border. Sew the 3" x 19¼" brown print strips to the top and bottom of the quilt top and press.

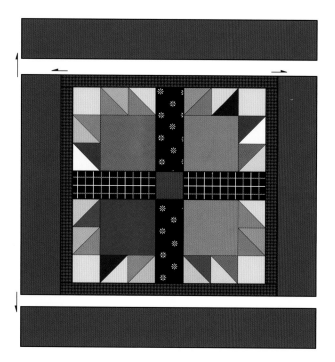

Finishing the Quilt

1. Layer the quilt top, batting, and backing, and baste the layers together as shown in "Putting the Quilt Together" on page 75.

2. Quilt a large X in each sashing strip and quilt in the ditch around each patch. Quilt diagonal lines through the block squares and at the border corners, and quilt straight lines at regular intervals across the width of the borders.

3. Attach the maroon print binding to the quilt, referring to "Single-Fold Binding" on page 76.

COURAGE THROUGH ADVERSITY

"O Mary I have not wrote you half of the truble we have had but I hav Wrote you anuf to let you now that you dont now whattruble is."

—Virginia Reed, age 12, survivor of the ill-fated Donner party whose members suffered great tragedy when they took a cutoff to make up for lost time

DEATH WAS NO STRANGER to the pioneers. The loss of a loved one was a common occurrence. Children lost one or both parents and parents lost children. In her book *I Walked to Zion,* Susan Arrington Madsen notes, "For many, it was a first and agonizing encounter with the reality of death. Adolescents stood in stunned silence as graves were dug for their parents, a sibling, or a beloved playmate."

The death toll on the trail was so high that we don't even have all the numbers. Many journals are filled with accounts of grave markers passed on the trip. Martha Read's diary from 1852 gives us an idea of just how much death the travelers were confronted with on a daily basis:

"Wdns. June 9. Traveled 20 miles. . . . Passed 12 graves. Campt on the bank of the river.

"Thurs. June 10. Traveled 10 miles. Burried

another woman out of our company tonight, a young man is not expected to live. . . . We passed 6 graves today. Weather warm but rather windy.

"Sat. June 12. Traveled 20 miles. . . . Saw 8 graves today.

"Sun. June 13. Traveled 25 miles. . . . Passe[d] 8 graves.

"Tues. June 15. Traveled 21 miles. . . . Passed 12 graves today. Campt near the river."

Pioneer families faced tremendous difficulties every day and every day had to rely on their instincts and experience to overcome these hardships. Spring weather proved to be a huge deterrent on the trail, bringing rainstorms, damaging winds, and perilous lightning. The strength of spirit we attribute to the pioneers may well have come from the self-assurance they achieved in repeatedly facing such obstacles and finding ways to surmount them.

Although many of the travelers had heard stories of and feared encounters with snakes, wolves, and other creatures of the wilderness, as well as ruthless Indian attacks and massacres, these incidents were rare. More lives were lost to disease and accidents than anything else.

Children fell out of wagons and were crushed by the huge wheels; some fell into the rivers when the wagons attempted a rocky crossing. Sallie Hester wrote about just how dangerous the trip could be:

"June 21. Left camp and started over . . . the worst road in the world. Have again struck the Platte [River] and followed it until we came to the ferry. Here we had a great deal of trouble swimming our cattle across, taking our wagons to pieces, unloading and replacing our traps. A number of accidents happened here. A lady and four children were drowned through the carelessness of those in charge of the ferry."

For most, however, the greatest threat lay in contracting an illness on the trail. Diseases such as cholera, dysentery, smallpox, and typhus took the lives of countless adults as well as children. Due largely to the unsanitary conditions of life on the trail, and a certain lack of knowledge about good health practices, these highly contagious diseases spread quickly throughout the wagon trains.

Mourning quilts were expressions of loss and sorrow, and emotional healing was hastened perhaps by the comfort of making a quilt. Pieces of clothing from the deceased were sometimes included in the quilt as reminders of and tributes to the departed.

Despite their hardships and trials, little seemed to daunt the spirits of these men, women, and children. For the many who were lost, many more survived through faith and perseverance, their happiness intact. Parthenia Blank, a teenager who witnessed up close the sufferings of other families, wrote, with a grateful heart: "June 20 [1852] Sunday This is a beautiful morning very warm did not expect to travel any to day a few sweet birds are singing and all nature seems to be praising their Maker. . . . We have great reason to be thankful for the many blessings and mercies that daily attend us Through dangers both seen and unseen the hand of God has directed us and while we see so many continually falling around us We still live in the enjoyment of good health and spirits."

Women sometimes brought along quilts for the journey that were intended to comfort the sick and shroud the dead. Ettie Scott remembers the grave of her mother: "The rolling hills were ablaze with beautiful wild roses . . . and we heaped and covered mother's grave with the lovely roses, so the cruel stones were hid from view." This little mourning quilt serves as a memorial to the many men, women, and children who died on the trail. ✎

Materials

Yardages are based on 42"-wide, 100%-cotton fabrics.

- ◆ ⅛ yard *each* or scraps of 9 black prints for blocks
- ◆ ⅛ yard *each* or scraps of 9 light prints for blocks
- ◆ ⅜ yard of dark floral print for outer border
- ◆ ¼ yard of dark print for sashing and inner border
- ◆ Scraps of 9 medium prints for blocks
- ◆ ¼ yard of black print for binding
- ◆ ⅞ yard of fabric for backing
- ◆ 29" x 29" piece of cotton batting

Cutting

From *each* of the 9 light prints, cut:

- ◆ 2 squares, 2⅞" x 2⅞" (18 squares total)

From *each* of the 9 black prints for blocks, cut:

- ◆ 2 squares, 2⅞" x 2⅞" (18 squares total)
- ◆ 5 squares, 1½" x 1½" (45 squares total)

From 1 black print, cut:

- ◆ 4 squares, 1½" x 1½"

From *each* of the 9 medium prints, cut:

- ◆ 4 squares, 1½" x 1½" (36 squares total)

From the dark print, cut:

- ◆ 4 strips, 1½" x 42"; crosscut into:
  - · 12 pieces, 1½" x 5½"
  - · 2 pieces, 1½" x 17½"
  - · 2 pieces, 1½" x 19½"

From the dark floral print, cut:

- ◆ 3 strips, 3½" x 42"; crosscut into 2 pieces, 3½" x 19½", and 2 pieces, 3½" x 25½"

From the black print for binding, cut:

- ◆ 3 strips, 1½" x 42"

Assembly

Each block consists of one light print, one medium print, and three different black prints. It's easiest if you select fabric for each block before you begin stitching the blocks together.

1. Draw a diagonal line from corner to corner on the wrong side of each 2⅞" light print square. Layer two matching marked squares on top of two matching 2⅞" black print squares, right sides together. Stitch ¼" from the line on both sides, and cut on the drawn line. Press the seams toward the darker fabric. Make 36 half-square-triangle units, four each from the nine different prints.

Make 36
in matching
sets of 4.

2. Sew four matching 1½" black print squares and four matching 1½" medium print squares together into pairs. Press toward the darker fabric. Make 36.

Make 36
in matching
sets of 4.

3. Sew two matching units from step 2 together with four matching half-square-triangle units from step 1, as shown. Make 9 pairs. Be sure to pair step 1 and step 2 units that feature a different black print.

Make 9 pairs.

4. Sew two matching units from step 2 together with a 1½" square of a different black print as shown, pressing the seams toward the black squares.

Make 9.

5. Sew two matching units from step 3 together with the matching unit from step 4 to make the Cross block. Press the seams as shown. Make nine blocks.

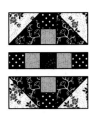

Make 9.

6. Sew three blocks together with two 1½" x 5½" dark print sashing pieces to make a row. Press toward the sashing. Make three rows.

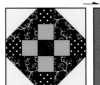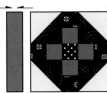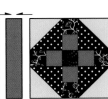

Make 3 rows.

7. Sew three 1½" x 5½" dark print sashing pieces together with two 1½" black print squares to make a sashing row. Press toward the sashing. Make two.

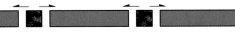

Make 2.

8. Sew the block rows and the sashing rows together, pressing seams toward the sashing rows.

9. Add the 1½" x 17½" dark print strips to the sides of the quilt top, pressing toward the border. Sew the 1½" x 19½" dark print strips to the top and bottom of the quilt top. Press seams toward the border.

10. Sew the 3½" x 19½" dark floral strips to the sides of the quilt top. Press seams toward the outer border. Add the 3½" x 25½" dark floral strips to the top and bottom of the quilt top, pressing seams toward the outer border.

Quilt Finishing

1. Layer the quilt top, batting, and backing, and baste the layers together as shown in "Putting the Quilt Together" on page 75.

2. Quilt in the ditch around each block; quilt a cross within the crosses. Quilt in the borders as desired.

3. Attach the black print binding to the quilt, referring to "Single-Fold Binding" on page 76.

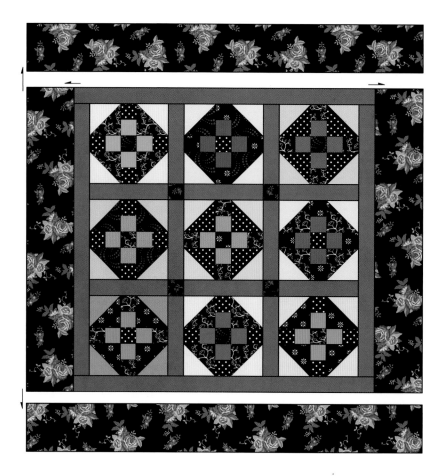

Making a New Home

"Our house has but one room." —Harriet Hitchcock, age 13

ONCE THE WAGON TRAINS STOPPED and the destinations had been reached, the hard work of making a new home began. Contrary to popular thought, the first structures built on the prairie were not always log cabins. Trees were scarce and only those families that settled near wooded areas were able to cut down trees and use the logs for houses. On the prairie, many homes were made of sod, quickly and easily built into the sides of hills. Sod homes were cool in the summer and warm in winter, although they lacked sunlight and didn't withstand rainy weather very well. These were temporary homes, and later, when they could afford the lumber, most settlers built larger, clapboard houses for their families.

The first job many pioneer women tackled was figuring out how to make their rough-hewn houses into homes. The primitive conditions under which many families lived would be unthinkable to us today. While many women were easily discouraged by the desolation of their new lives on the prairie, most worked hard to make life comfortable and civilized for their loved ones. Some families brought along furniture, pianos, and sewing machines, and those that didn't collected new possessions when they could afford to. Quilts in a cabin added tremendously to the comfort of home.

Husbands and wives worked as teams out of necessity to ensure their survival. By most accounts, the women were vital to the success of the farm. They not only tended to the indoor work of making a household run smoothly, but they also shared the load of physical labor and farming chores. Children played a crucial role as well. According to Marilyn Holt, author of *Children of the Western Plains,* "Children were viable, necessary contributors to the settlement process. They were the reason for building schools and organizing Sunday schools."

The designs of quilts at this time were simple and practical because families needed bedding in a hurry. While more complex patterns were being published in newspapers and magazines on the East Coast, new patterns were hard to come by on the frontier and many women shared their favorite blocks with new neighbors and traded quilting ideas learned from friends in other parts of the country.

Quilts from this time were decidedly scrappy. Pioneer women had to make do with what was available and so they often used old clothing and salvaged scraps for their quilts. Women were sometimes dependent on fleece from their own flocks, which was then carded, spun, and woven—hence the term "homespun." Roots of plants and vegetables, as well as berries and tree bark, were then used to dye those fabrics.

We tend to think of this period in American history as a simple, uncomplicated time and it is easy to idealize the lives of the pioneer women, forgetting the drudgery to which they were subjected. Quilts had to be made as quickly as possible in what little time the women were afforded. Forming a community of quilters helped tremendously, both in spirit and in the actual physical work of making the quilts. The piecing of quilts took place alone, but the quilting itself became a group effort of friends and neighbors.

For the children, it was a time of new beginnings— there was excitement mixed with anxiety and shock at what they were expected to call home. Far from life in a town, children had to adapt to living with snakes and other wild animals. Life may not have been as solitary as it was for the women, however, since most families were large and there was always an abundance of siblings to help ease any loneliness.

In warm weather, the children found pleasure outside, exploring the prairie with its wondrous flowers and strange little animals. This was not a life of tea parties and fancy socials, except in the child's world of play. The only tea parties that took place on the frontier at that time may have been the gatherings children held with their dolls, so primitive were the pioneers' surroundings at first.

Day-to-day life on the prairie would not have been the most pleasant experience. Despite the odds, despite their many ordeals, the settlers' strength and courage, coupled with a hopeful enthusiasm, carried them through. Little by little, through hard work and determination, the wilderness was domesticated and life on the American frontier was forever changed.

LOG CABIN QUILT

One of the most familiar and beloved of quilt patterns from the nineteenth century has to be the Log Cabin block. This little quilt, with its light and dark strips resembling the logs in a cabin, is a perfect symbol of rugged pioneer life on the prairie. ≈

Materials

Yardages are based on 42"-wide, 100%-cotton fabrics.

✦ ⅛ yard *each* or scraps of 6 to 12 dark prints for blocks

✦ ⅛ yard *each* or scraps of 6 to 12 light prints for blocks

✦ ⅛ yard *total* or scraps of 4 to 6 pink prints for block centers

✦ ¼ yard of medium print for binding

✦ ½ yard of fabric for backing

✦ 17" x 22" piece of cotton batting

Cutting

If you want the "logs" around the center square to match (forming an L shape), you will need to cut the pieces in pairs from each fabric. For example, cut a 2"-long and a 2½"-long piece from the same light print and cut a 2½"-long and a 3"-long piece from the same dark print.

From the pink prints, cut:

✦ 12 squares, 2" x 2"

From the light prints, cut:

✦ 12 pieces, 1" x 2"
✦ 12 pieces, 1" x 2½"
✦ 12 pieces, 1" x 3"
✦ 12 pieces, 1" x 3½"
✦ 12 pieces, 1" x 4"
✦ 12 pieces, 1" x 4½"

From the dark prints, cut:

✦ 12 pieces, 1" x 2½"
✦ 12 pieces, 1" x 3"
✦ 12 pieces, 1" x 3½"
✦ 12 pieces, 1" x 4"
✦ 12 pieces, 1" x 4½"
✦ 12 pieces, 1" x 5"

From the medium print, cut:

✦ 2 strips, 1½" x 42"

Assembly

1. Starting with a 2" pink square, sew a 1" x 2" light print piece to one side. Press away from the center. Rotate the unit so that the just-added piece is on top. Add a second light print piece, 1" x 2½", to the right side of the unit. Press all the newly added pieces away from the center.

2. Rotate the block again and add a 1" x 2½" dark print piece to the right side. Press. Turn and add the next dark print piece, 1" x 3". Press. Continue adding pieces or "logs" in this way, alternating two light and two dark fabrics until you have three sets of light logs and three sets of dark logs, ending with the dark print.

Plan a Mistake

If you want to give your quilt the look of having been made by a child, you can include an intentional "mistake" block. Simply add the first dark print log to the wrong side of the center block as you're piecing.

3. Trim and square up the block, if needed, so that it measures 5" x 5". Make 12 blocks.

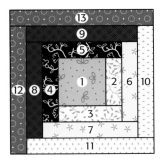

Make 12.

4. Arrange the blocks as shown. Sew together four rows of three blocks each, pressing seams in the opposite direction from row to row. Sew the rows together and press the seams in one direction.

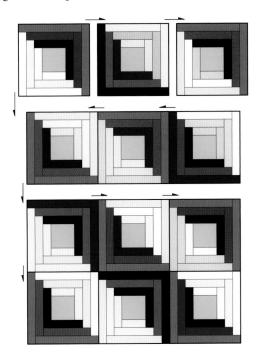

Finishing the Quilt

1. Layer the quilt top, batting, and backing, and baste the layers together as shown in "Putting the Quilt Together" on page 75.

2. Quilt in the ditch around each strip.

3. Attach the medium print binding to the quilt, referring to "Single-Fold Binding" on page 76.

BRAIDED DOLL RUG

Nothing went to waste on the prairie. Leftover fabric strips from clothing and other scraps were sewn together and then braided to make colorful rugs that brought a bit of warmth and coziness to dreary frontier cabins. ⌒

Materials

Yardages are based on 42"-wide, 100%-cotton fabrics.

+ ¼ yard *each* of 3 prints

Cutting

From *each* of the 3 prints, cut:

+ 2 strips, 1" x 42" (6 strips total)

Assembly

1. Sew the matching strips of each print together with a diagonal seam. Trim the seam allowance to ¼" and press the seam open. Fold each strip in half lengthwise with wrong sides together and press lightly.

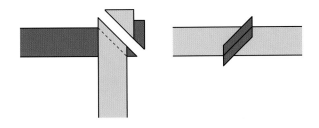

2. Unfold and sew two different fabric strips together with a diagonal seam; trim as before. Refold the strips and insert the third strip inside the fold to make a T formation. Stitch together.

3. Anchor the strips where they are joined by taping them tightly to the edge of a table or the back of a chair, or by inserting them into a tightly closed drawer. Braid the strips together, folding (rather than twisting) the strips over each other as you braid to preserve the folds in each strip and make the braid lie flat. Don't pull too tightly; you want the braid to be flexible and curve easily.

4. Working on a hard, flat surface, coil the braided strip into a circular shape (or oval if you prefer). Do not coil too tightly or the rug will not lie flat. Pin the braid together as you coil to maintain its circular shape.

5. Tuck the end under the rug and snip off any threads from the edges of the fabric.

Tuck end under rug.

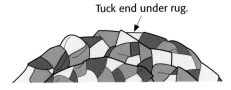

6. With a neutral-colored thread, stitch the coils together. Press lightly with an iron set on steam to shape the rug. You can use a seam ripper to tuck unfinished ends under or manipulate the right and wrong sides of the fabric strips as needed.

ONE LAND, MANY CULTURES

"The Indians are quite numerous. Now and again they ride by on their ponies. . . .
I fear we will have trouble with them, but hope for the best."

—Lucretia Epperson, 1864

WESTWARD EXPANSION affected the lives of Native Americans more than any other culture during that time. Guidebooks written to advise westward travelers warned about the "natives" and filled the pioneers with anxiety and fear before any encounters even took place. American Indians were viewed as troublesome and dangerous, but it is a myth that they killed a great many settlers on the trail west—far more deaths occurred from disease and accidents. More often than not, the Native Americans reacted to the white travelers with curious observation rather than hostile action.

The Native American customs and manners were so different from their own that many white settlers were suspicious and afraid. The mistrust and fear ultimately came from a lack of understanding of the cultural differences between the two groups.

The Native Americans had no words in their language for "land ownership." In their view, the land, like the air, belonged to everyone, and their culture did not support the concept of private claims on it. Cultures clashed and Native American lives were changed forever when the white settlers arrived on those lands and claimed them as their own. With the movement west, homelands of the American Indians were trampled and buffalo herds destroyed, all in violation of government promises to respect the boundaries set aside for the various tribes.

Stories of Indian massacres and abductions aside, fear was probably the pioneers' worst enemy. Many settlers never had any encounters with Native Americans, and those who did often had peaceful interactions.

For African Americans in the nineteenth century, the West was viewed as the doorway to opportunities denied during slavery—opportunities for prosperity and a hope for a better future, in addition to the search for equality. Yet despite their release from slavery, black Americans still had to face strong discrimination and cultural prejudices on the frontier.

Although few quilts survived, those made by African-American women during this time are striking examples of their struggle for individuality and expression. We see in the quilts the bright colors of hopefulness and optimism about the future, mixed with strong African conventions of weaving and textile traditions. Made from scraps, the quilts exhibited bold designs that reaffirmed each quilter's individuality—something slavery could not take away. Many of the quilts embodied a sense of freedom and depicted a strong departure from traditional quilting styles. Quilters today are finally recognizing the true sense of expression through color that these African-American quilts brought to American quilting traditions.

Asians in the West were treated much like the Native Americans and African Americans, discriminated against for their cultural differences. Yet the influence of this group was felt strongly across the nation. The Chinese and Japanese immigrants were instrumental in building the railroads that linked the East Coast to the West Coast in the latter part of the nineteenth century. Lured by hopes of prosperity in the United States, many immigrants fled poor farming and economic conditions in their own countries. Hoping to seek their fortunes and return to their homeland, many instead settled on the West Coast and established roots for their families there.

Facing the same challenges as the pioneers but with the struggles multiplied by the experience of living among people with different customs and often an unfamiliar language, people in these groups did not have an easy life. With their "strange" customs and languages, they were often considered threats to the American culture, yet were assimilated into society over the years. Though it has been slow in coming, Americans have been able to admit the mistakes of the past and welcome the diversity and customs that different people contribute to the culture of our country. Like a patchwork quilt, the merging of different cultures and peoples helped to make America the melting pot it is today.

NATIVE AMERICAN QUILT

The pioneers' fears about and prejudices against "Indians" tainted their encounters with the Native Americans. More often than not, those encounters were peaceful and even extremely helpful to the settlers. This colorful little quilt was inspired by the many traditional patterns found on Native American baskets, woven blankets, and rugs.

Materials

Yardages are based on 42"-wide, 100%-cotton fabrics.

- ¼ yard of gold print for blocks
- ¼ yard of medium blue print for setting square and triangles
- ⅛ yard of red print for blocks
- ⅛ yard of indigo print for blocks
- ⅛ yard of dark green print for border
- ⅛ yard of tan print for border
- ¼ yard of red plaid for binding
- ⅝ yard of fabric for backing
- 21" x 21" piece of cotton batting
- Red quilting thread

Cutting

From the gold print, cut:
- 12 squares, 2⅜" x 2⅜"
- 8 squares, 2" x 2"

From the red print, cut:
- 6 squares, 2⅜" x 2⅜"
- 2 squares, 2" x 2"

From the indigo print, cut:
- 6 squares, 2⅜" x 2⅜"
- 2 squares, 2" x 2"

From the medium blue print, cut:
- 1 square, 5" x 5"
- 2 squares, 4⅛" x 4⅛"; cut each square in half diagonally once
- 1 square, 7⅝" x 7⅝"; cut in half diagonally twice

From the dark green print, cut:
- 1 strip, 2½" x 42"; crosscut into 2 pieces, 2½" x 13¼"

From the tan print, cut:
- 1 strip, 2½" x 42"; crosscut into 2 pieces, 2½" x 17¼"

From the red plaid, cut:
- 2 strips, 1½" x 42"

Assembly

1. Draw a diagonal line from corner to corner on the wrong side of each 2⅜" gold square. Layer a marked gold square on each 2⅜" red square and each 2⅜" indigo square, right sides together. Stitch ¼" from the line on both sides. Cut on the drawn line to make 12 half-square-triangle units of each color combination. Press seam allowances toward the darker fabric.

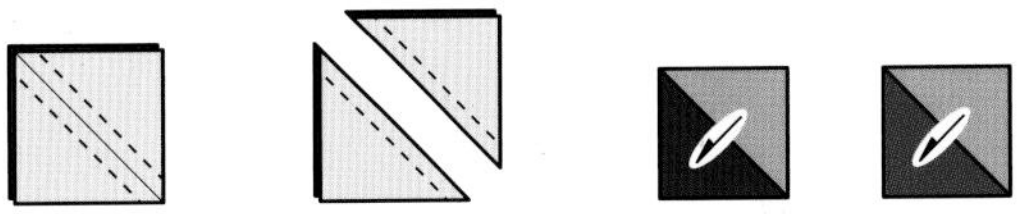

Make 12.   Make 12.

2. Arrange six indigo-and-gold units from step 1, a 2" red square, and two 2" gold squares in three rows as shown. Sew the units into rows, pressing seams in the opposite direction from row to row. Sew the rows together. Make two blocks.

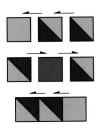

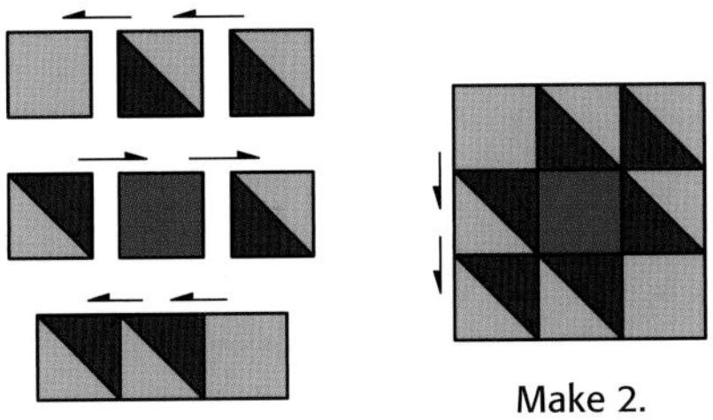

Make 2.

3. Arrange six red-and-gold units from step 1, a 2" indigo square, and two 2" gold squares in three rows as shown. Sew the units into rows, pressing seams in the opposite direction from row to row. Sew the rows together. Make two blocks.

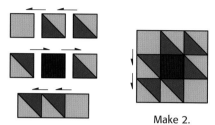

Make 2.

4. Arrange the blocks, the 5" medium blue square, and the setting triangles in diagonal rows as shown. Sew the diagonal rows, pressing away from the pieced blocks. Add the corner triangles and sew the rows together.

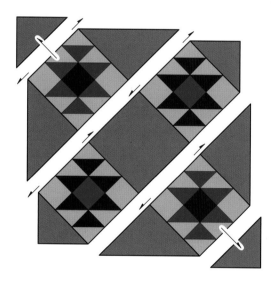

5. Trim and square up the quilt top, leaving ¼" beyond the points of the blocks.

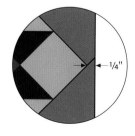

¼"

6. Sew the 2½" x 13¼" green print strips to the top and bottom of the quilt top. Press seams toward the border. Add the 2½" x 17¼" tan print strips to the sides of the quilt top, pressing seams toward the border.

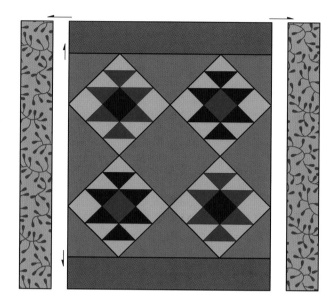

Finishing the Quilt

1. Layer the quilt top, batting, and backing, and baste the layers together as shown in "Putting the Quilt Together" on page 75.

2. Quilt in the ditch around each block and outline the indigo and red pieces with red quilting thread. Quilt four on-point squares in the central medium blue square, bisecting the two side squares with vertical lines through the center. Quilt triangles in the medium blue side setting triangles.

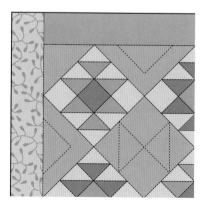

3. Attach the red plaid binding to the quilt, referring to "Single-Fold Binding" on page 76.

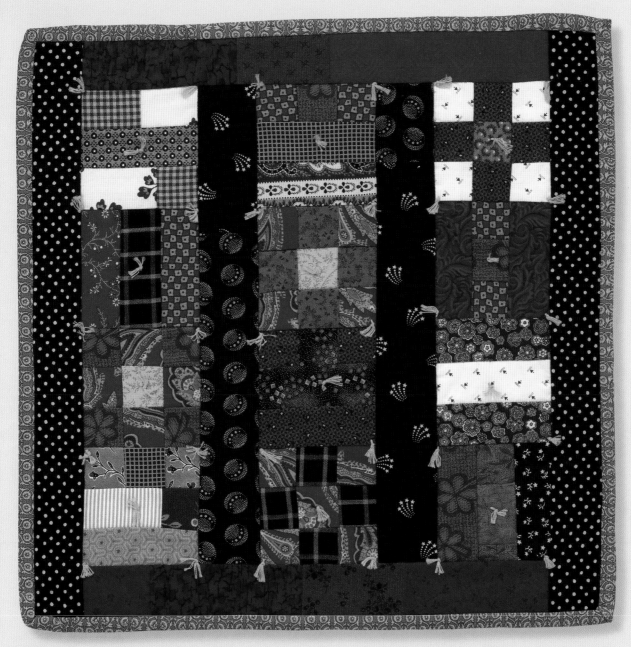

African-American quilts from the nineteenth century were noted for their eclectic style, obviously influenced by African design traditions. Bold colors and asymmetrical piecing frequently characterized these quilts. Because the quilts were made in a hurry, often after a long workday in the fields, tying them with yarn or thread was a way of eliminating the need to spend time quilting the three layers together.

Materials

Yardages are based on 42"-wide, 100%-cotton fabrics.

- ⅛ yard *each* of 2 different indigo prints for sashing
- ⅛ yard of indigo polka-dot print for border
- Scraps of 25 to 30 light, bright, and dark prints for blocks
- Scraps of 6 to 8 red prints for pieced border
- ¼ yard of poison green print for binding
- ⅝ yard of fabric for backing
- 18" x 18" piece of cotton batting
- 1 skein of yellow embroidery floss
- Large-eye needle

Cutting

From the scraps of light, bright, and dark prints, cut:
- 20 strips, 1½" wide and in varying lengths from 3" to 12"

From *each* of the indigo prints for sashing, cut:
- 1 piece, 2" x 12" (2 pieces total)
- 1 piece, 2" x 6" (2 pieces total)

From the red prints, cut:
- 6 to 8 pieces, 1¾" wide and in random lengths from 2½" to 6"

From the indigo polka-dot print, cut:
- 1 strip, 1¾" x 42"; crosscut into 2 pieces, 1¾" x 15"

From the poison green print, cut:
- 2 strips, 1½" x 42"

Assembly

This little quilt consists of a dozen blocks—four Nine Patch blocks, two Rail Fence blocks, and six randomly pieced Rail Fence Variation blocks.

1. For each Nine Patch block, cut the following pieces from the light, bright, and dark 1½" strips: two sets of four matching 1½" squares and one contrasting 1½" square for the center. Sew the squares together into rows as shown to make a 3½" unfinished block. Press. Repeat to make four blocks.

Make 4.

2. For each Rail Fence block, cut three 1½" x 3½" rectangles and sew them together as shown. Press. Make two blocks.

Make 2.

3. To make the Rail Fence Variation blocks, use the pieces cut from light, bright, and dark scraps. Randomly cut and sew together 1½"-wide pieces of varying lengths to make 18 strips, 3½" long. Sew three strips together to make a 3½" square block. Press. Make six blocks.

Make 6.

4. Sew four blocks together into a vertical row as shown. Make three rows.

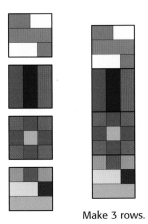

Make 3 rows.

5. Sew each 2" x 12" indigo sashing piece to a 2" x 6" piece of the other indigo print. Press. The strips are longer than necessary and will be trimmed in the next step.

Make 2.

6. Place the two indigo sashing strips between the block rows. Stagger the position of the seams for a random appearance, and trim the strips to 12½". Sew the strips and rows together. Press toward the sashing.

7. For the top and bottom borders, sew together the 1¾" red print pieces to make two strips, 12½" long. Sew to the top and bottom of the quilt top. Press toward the border.

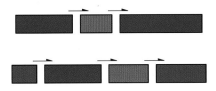

8. Sew the 1¾" x 15" indigo polka-dot strips to the sides of the quilt top. Press toward the border.

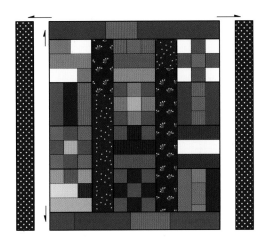

Finishing the Quilt

1. Layer the quilt top, batting, and backing, and baste the layers together as shown in "Putting the Quilt Together" on page 75.

2. Tie the quilt using a large-eye needle and six strands of yellow embroidery floss through all three layers. Tie knots in the corners and the center of each block, clipping the ends of the floss to about ¼".

3. Attach the poison green print binding to the quilt, referring to "Single-Fold Binding" on page 76.

FAMILY LIFE: WORK AND PLAY

"Ma was busy, too. Laura and Mary helped her weed the garden, and they helped her feed the calves and the hens. They gathered the eggs, and they helped make cheese."

—Laura Ingalls Wilder, from *Little House in the Big Woods*

P EOPLE IN THE nineteenth century were accustomed to hard work, and children were not exempt from it. Physical labor was an inevitable part of life on the frontier. The family was a work unit—children were relied upon as a source of labor and were expected to do their part in the daily workload. Children as young as four could feed the chickens and gather plants and berries; older children helped with the laundry, cooking, sewing, and minding the younger ones.

While hard work was an inescapable part of life on the frontier, the pioneers made time for relaxation, too. Children on the prairie were uninhibited by the restrictions that city life entailed. They were often free to explore their new surroundings and many turned to imaginative play because of limited toys and resources.

Favorite activities for both boys and girls included fishing and swimming in the summer and ice skating and sledding in the winter.

Many photos of young girls from this time period show them posed with their dolls. Perhaps that tells us what an important role dolls played in the children's lives. The cloth doll was a favorite companion and, along with other dolls that youngsters brought with them, may have given comfort when needed, in the same way that quilts gave comfort and warmth in the new environment.

If life was lonely, then quilting bees, or quiltings, as they were sometimes called, provided a measure of fun to ease that loneliness and were an eagerly awaited social activity. Church was a viable source of social contacts and gave a sense of community to pioneers who eagerly took part in activities like socials, dances, and picnics that the church offered.

Quilting flourished in nineteenth-century America. Frontier life must have presented more than enough challenges for pioneer women, but perhaps that very environment helped contribute to the growing importance of quilting. Having no other outlet for creativity, women turned to quilting as one of their first forms of artistic expression while still keeping within functional boundaries. The first quilt a young girl made was often a simple one for a doll, and the piecing and quilting grew more complex as girls became more adept at the craft.

The nineteenth-century American work ethic was very strong. Alongside the women, the girls did their daily chores. Cooking, cleaning, and sewing and mending clothes all helped prepare a girl for eventually running a household and having a family. Looking after younger siblings often forced the girls into mothering roles at early ages. When mothers became too weak for work after an illness or childbirth, some young girls' childhoods were interrupted as they took on adult responsibilities.

Yet child's play was considered important, especially later in the century, as Americans began to place more value on childhood. Girls were encouraged to play with dolls in order to develop their nurturing potential and as a way to train them for future motherhood roles. Children gained a sense of confidence in their value through the skills they obtained.

To say the least, frontier living was oftentimes difficult and dreary. Today, it is easy for us to glorify the American frontier and the simple life it embodied. These men, women, and children were hardworking beyond our imaginations. And, although sometimes the days seemed overfilled with chores, pioneer families still made time in their busy lives for recreational activities that strengthened family bonds.

Although daily life was packed with work and chores, pioneer families made time for fun and games. This little quilt is reminiscent of the early wooden game boards so common in the nineteenth century and treasured as folk-art pieces today.

Materials

Yardages are based on 42"-wide, 100%-cotton fabrics.

- ⅜ yard *total* or scraps of assorted blue prints for blocks and outer border
- ¼ yard *total* or scraps of assorted red prints for blocks and outer border
- ¼ yard *total* or scraps of assorted light prints for blocks and border corner squares
- ⅛ yard of red print for inner border
- ¼ yard of dark blue print for binding
- ⅝ yard of fabric for backing
- 20" x 20" piece of cotton batting

Cutting

From the assorted blue prints, cut:
- 104 squares, 1¾" x 1¾"
- 2 squares, 3⅜" x 3⅜"

From the assorted light prints, cut:
- 32 squares, 1¾" x 1¾"
- 2 squares, 3⅜" x 3⅜"

From the red print for inner border, cut:
- 1 strip, 1⅛" x 42"; crosscut into 2 pieces, 1⅛" x 10½", and 2 pieces, 1⅛" x 11¾"

From the assorted red prints, cut:
- 36 rectangles, 1¾" x 3"

From the dark blue print for binding, cut:
- 2 strips, 1½" x 42"

Assembly

1. Sew a 1¾" blue print square together with a 1¾" light print square. Press toward the dark fabric. Make 32. Sew one unit to another as shown, creating a Four Patch block. Press. Make 16.

Make 16.

2. Sew the blocks together into four rows of four blocks each, pressing seams in the opposite direction from row to row.

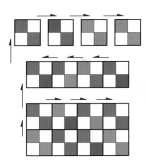

3. Sew the rows together and press the seams in one direction.

4. Sew the 1⅛" x 10½" red print strips to the sides of the quilt top. Press toward the border. Sew the 1⅛" x 11¾" red print strips to the top and bottom of the quilt top and press.

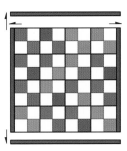

5. Draw a diagonal line from corner to corner on the wrong side of each 3⅜" light print square. Place a marked square on top of a 3⅜" blue print square. Sew ¼" from the line on both sides. Cut on the drawn line. Repeat to make four half-square-triangle units. Press and set aside.

Make 4.

6. To make the flying-geese units for the outer border, draw a diagonal line on the wrong side of each of the 72 remaining 1¾" blue squares. Layer a marked blue square on one end of a 1¾" x 3" red print rectangle, right sides together, as shown. Sew on the line and trim to a ¼" seam allowance. Press the triangle toward the corner. Place a second marked blue square on the other end of the rectangle, right sides together, with the diagonal line oriented in the opposite direction from the first piece. Stitch on the drawn line. Trim to a ¼" seam allowance and press toward the corner. Make a total of 36 flying-geese units.

Make 36.

7. Join nine flying-geese units to form a strip, with triangle points facing in the same direction. Make four border strips. Press the seams as shown.

Make 4.

8. Stitch two flying-geese strips to the sides of the quilt top, pressing toward the inner border.

9. Sew a half-square-triangle unit from step 5 to each end of the two remaining flying-geese strips, as shown. Sew these units to the top and bottom of the quilt top, matching seams at the corners. Press.

Finishing the Quilt

1. Layer the quilt top, batting, and backing, and baste the layers together as shown in "Putting the Quilt Together" on page 75.

2. Quilt diagonal lines through the squares of the checkerboard. Quilt in the ditch around the triangle points and along the red inner border.

3. Attach the dark blue print binding to the quilt, referring to "Single-Fold Binding" on page 76.

PRAIRIE BASKETS QUILT

As the West was being settled, the hills and prairies were filled with berries of all kinds growing in the wild. From an early age, children were expected to help out with chores. Berry picking was a suitable task for the youngest children as well as a favorite pastime for older ones. ⌇

Materials

Yardages are based on 42"-wide, 100%-cotton fabrics.

- ¼ yard of chrome yellow print for blocks and inner border
- ¼ yard of small-scale indigo print for blocks and setting pieces
- ¼ yard of medium-scale indigo print for outer border
- ¼ yard of dark blue check for binding
- ⅝ yard of fabric for backing
- 20" x 20" piece of cotton batting
- Yellow quilting thread

Tea Dyeing

If you are unable to find chrome yellow fabric, tea dye some bright yellow fabric from your stash. Simply place two to three tea bags in a glass bowl, add boiling water, wait until the water is lukewarm, and then add the yellow fabric. Rinse the fabric carefully, dry it, and then press it before cutting. ✎

Cutting

From the chrome yellow print, cut:

- 12 squares, 1⅞" x 1⅞"; cut 4 squares in half diagonally once to yield 8 triangles
- 2 squares, 2⅞" x 2⅞"
- 2 strips, 1" x 42"

From the small-scale indigo print, cut:

- 8 squares, 1⅞" x 1⅞"
- 4 squares, 2⅞" x 2⅞"; cut 2 squares in half diagonally once to yield 4 triangles
- 8 rectangles, 1½" x 2½"
- 4 squares, 1½" x 1½"
- 1 square, 4½" x 4½"
- 2 squares, 3¾" x 3¾"; cut each square in half diagonally once
- 1 square, 7" x 7"; cut in half diagonally twice

From the medium-scale indigo print, cut:

- 2 strips, 2½" x 42"

From the dark blue check, cut:

- 2 strips, 1½" x 42"

Assembly

1. Draw a diagonal line from corner to corner on the wrong side of the eight 1⅞" yellow squares. Layer each marked square on top of a 1⅞" indigo square, right sides together. Sew ¼" from the line on both sides. Cut on the drawn line and press. Make 16 half-square-triangle units.

Make 16.

2. Draw a diagonal line from corner to corner on the wrong side of each 2⅞" yellow square. Place a marked square on top of a 2⅞" indigo square, right sides together. Sew ¼" from the line on both sides. Cut on the drawn line and press. Make four half-square-triangle units.

Make 4.

3. Sew a yellow triangle cut from the 1⅞" squares to the end of a 1½" x 2½" indigo rectangle as shown. Make four of each unit.

Make 4.   Make 4.

4. Arrange and sew one 1½" indigo square, four half-square-triangle units from step 1, and one half-square-triangle unit from step 2 as shown. Press. Make four.

Make 4.

5. Sew two side units from step 3 to a unit from step 4. Add a triangle cut from the 2⅞" indigo squares. Press as shown. Make four.

Make 4.

6. Lay out the Basket blocks, the 4½" indigo square, and the side and corner setting triangles. Sew the blocks and setting pieces together into rows. Press the seams toward the setting pieces.

7. Sew the rows together as shown. Press toward the corner triangles.

8. Measure the length of the quilt through the center. Using a 1" x 42" yellow strip, cut two pieces to the measured length. Sew the pieces to the sides of the quilt top, and press toward the border. Measure the width of the quilt through the center, including the borders just added. Using the remaining 1" x 42" yellow strip, cut two pieces to that measurement and sew them to the top and bottom of the quilt top. Press toward the border.

9. Repeat the measuring procedure from step 8 to cut the 2½" medium-scale indigo border strips and sew them to the quilt. Press.

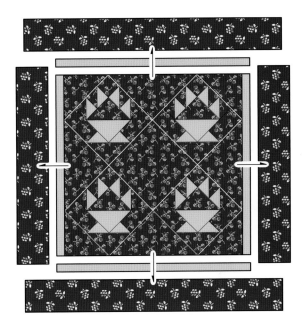

Finishing the Quilt

1. Layer the quilt top, batting, and backing, and baste the layers together as shown in "Putting the Quilt Together" on page 75.

2. With bright yellow quilting thread, quilt in the ditch around each block, diagonal lines through the center square, and a straight line through the middle of the border.

3. Attach the blue check binding to the quilt, referring to "Single-Fold Binding" on page 76.

PRAIRIE DOLL APRON

Young pioneer girls were expected to help their families as much as they were able. Some became "little mothers" at early ages and took on adult responsibilities such as cooking, cleaning, washing and mending clothes, and tending to the younger children when necessary. Little girls often wore aprons to protect their clothing, and their dolls may have worn them as well.

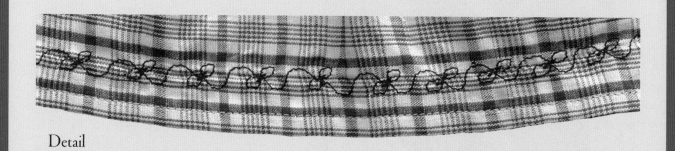

Detail

Materials

Yardages are based on 42"-wide, 100%-cotton fabrics.

+ 1 fat quarter of plaid fabric for apron skirt
+ ⅛ yard of red print for waistband and ties
+ Red thread

Cutting

From the plaid fabric, cut:

+ 1 rectangle, 8" x 10½"

From the red print, cut:

+ 1 strip, 2" x 25"

Assembly

1. Turn under the 8"-long sides and the lower edge of the plaid rectangle ⅛" and press. Turn under again ¼", press, and stitch to hem the edges.

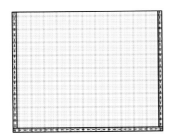

2. Using red thread and a decorative stitch on your sewing machine, stitch along the lower edge of the apron, approximately ½" from the bottom.

3. Machine baste two parallel rows across the top of the apron skirt, one a scant ¼" from the raw edge and the second ⅜" from the first row of stitching. Mark the center of the apron with a pencil along the top edge. Pull the gathering threads on either side to gather the skirt to approximately 6½". Set aside.

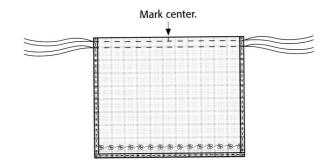

4. To make the waistband and ties, turn under the short ends of the red strip ¼", press, and topstitch. Turn under each long edge of the strip ¼" and press, but do not stitch.

5. With right sides together and raw edges even, pin the center of the waistband to the center of the apron skirt. Pin at the sides and in between. Sew along the fold line of the red strip, ¼" from the raw edges, across the gathers. Remove the basting thread.

6. Fold the waistband over the raw edge of the apron skirt, aligning the fold with the stitching line. Pin in place and press. Press the tie strips in half too so that the folded edges are aligned. Beginning at one end of the tie, stitch the folded edges together. Continue sewing across the waistband and along the folded edges of the other tie until you reach the end.

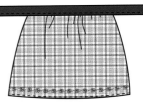

"Rode to Cache Creek on my pony to visit Bells school. . . . What a place for a school room A few rough benches . . . and Bell in the middle of the room presiding with matronly dignity. . . . There are no books . . . so Bell teaches them what she knows."

—Harriet Hitchcock, age 13

THE SCHOOLHOUSES were constructed soon after the land was cleared and the homes built. It was the women who were instrumental in setting up the first schools, churches, and libraries. Pioneer mothers knew the importance of education—intellectual as well as spiritual and moral—and were eager to spread literacy. Children were taught at home first, with the family Bible their only resource for learning reading and writing, but many parents soon realized their own limitations and the value of classroom instruction.

The schoolhouses served the dual purposes of education and religion, as the first church congregations usually met in these primitive buildings as well. In addition to food for the soul, churches provided valuable sources of information from other places. Members shared news from home and gave support to one another.

The schools also took on the role of social centers in the small towns that developed as the land was settled. Because life on the prairie could be so isolating—one's closest neighbors sometimes lived miles away—schools became much-needed social centers and meetinghouses that helped solidify a community. Everyone looked forward to social gatherings at the schoolhouses. Spelling bees and contests for best recitation of poetry or multiplication tables were such popular social diversions that even adults participated.

Teaching was one of the few career choices for women at that time and most who entered that profession were extremely dedicated. Some women came from the East on horseback or by wagon to take advantage of the teaching opportunities on the frontier, even though wages may have amounted to as little as one dollar per day. Additional compensation was provided in the form of room and board, and teachers often lodged with various families on a rotating basis.

So eager were the settlers for educational resources that sometimes all that was required of a teacher was that she know how to read and write. Girls in their teens were recruited whenever there was a lack of teachers to be found. In 1882, Laura Ingalls Wilder, author of the beloved *Little House* series of books, earned her teaching certificate and became a teacher in DeSmet, South Dakota, at the age of 15.

Today we idealize the one-room schoolhouse with images of rosy-cheeked children who traveled miles on foot to get to the nearest school, eager to learn. Although there may have been some warm fellowship in rural schools, in reality the classroom was cold and primitive, and students were not always enthused about being sent there to learn. The school day took up a large portion of the children's time, away from the farm, and most were held responsible for finishing their morning and afternoon chores as well. Younger children learned from the older ones, who often helped the teacher. Books were scarce and had to be shared among the students. When one child was learning arithmetic, another was studying geography so that the books could be rotated among them. Yet even with all the challenges, schooling on the frontier thrived over the years, through the pioneers' firm determination to educate their children and ensure better lives for future generations.

Little Red Schoolhouse Quilt

The old-fashioned pioneer schoolhouse was frequently a one-room building simply furnished with log benches and a fireplace or pot-bellied stove for warmth in the winter. The school building often served as the town church and meeting place for community events. The cherished Schoolhouse block has been a favorite of quiltmakers for years.

Materials

Yardages are based on 42"-wide, 100%-cotton fabrics.

- ⅜ yard of blue floral print for Hourglass blocks and border
- ¼ yard *or* 1 fat eighth of red polka-dot print for Hourglass blocks
- ¼ yard *or* 1 fat eighth of light tan print for Hourglass blocks
- ⅛ yard *each* or scraps of 5 light prints for Schoolhouse blocks
- ⅛ yard *each* or scraps of 4 red prints for Schoolhouse blocks
- ⅛ yard *or* scraps of medium blue print for Schoolhouse block
- Scraps of 4 different blue checks and prints for roofs
- Scrap of red check for roof
- ¼ yard of light print for binding
- ⅝ yard of fabric for backing
- 19" x 19" piece of cotton batting

Cutting

Make templates using the patterns on page 65.

From *each* of the 4 red prints, cut:
- 2 squares, 1" x 1" (8 squares total)
- 4 pieces, 1" x 2" (16 pieces total)
- 2 pieces, 1" x 2" (8 pieces total)
- 2 pieces, 1" x 3" (8 pieces total)
- 1 piece using template 2 (4 pieces total)

From *one* of the red prints, cut:
- 2 squares, 1" x 1"

From *each* of the 5 light prints, cut:
- 2 pieces, 1" x 1¼" (10 pieces total)
- 3 pieces, 1" x 2" (15 pieces total)
- 1 piece, 1" x 2½" (5 pieces total)
- 1 piece using template 1 (5 pieces total)
- 1 piece using template 1 reversed (5 pieces total)

From the medium blue print, cut:
- 4 pieces, 1" x 2"
- 2 pieces, 1" x 2½"
- 2 pieces, 1" x 3"
- 1 piece using template 2

From the red check, cut:
- 1 piece using template 3

From *each* of the 4 blue scraps, cut:
- 1 piece using template 3 (4 pieces total)

From the red polka-dot print, cut:
- 1 square, 5¼" x 5¼"; cut in half diagonally twice

From the light tan print, cut:
- 1 square, 5¼" x 5¼"; cut in half diagonally twice

From the blue floral print, cut:
- 2 squares, 5¼" x 5¼"; cut each square in half diagonally twice
- 2 strips, 2¼" x 42"; crosscut into 2 pieces, 2¼" x 12½", and 2 pieces, 2¼" x 16"

From the light print for binding, cut:
- 2 strips, 1½" x 42"

Assembly

1. To make a red Schoolhouse block, sew two matching 1" x 2½" red print pieces to the sides of a 1" x 2½" light print piece. Press toward the red print. Add a 1" x 2" red print piece to the top of the unit. Press and set aside.

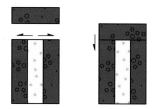

2. Sew three 1" x 2" red print pieces and two 1" x 2" light print pieces together as shown. Sew a 1" x 3" red print piece to the top and bottom of the unit, as shown. Press and set aside.

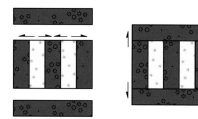

3. Sew two 1" red print squares, two 1" x 1¼" light print pieces, and a 1" x 2" light print piece together as shown. Press.

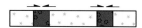

4. Using the pieces cut from templates, sew the roof and background pieces together as shown. Use a pin to align the dots at the seam intersections, and pin before sewing. Remove the pins as you get to them. Press.

5. Piece the block units together as shown. Repeat steps 1 through 5 to make four red schoolhouses with blue roofs, and one blue schoolhouse with a red-checked roof.

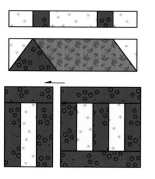
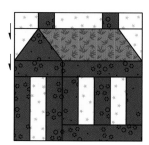

Make 4 red.

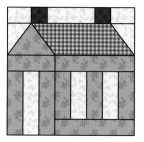

Make 1 blue.

6. To make the Hourglass blocks, sew a red polka-dot quarter-square triangle to a blue floral print quarter-square triangle, and a light print quarter-square triangle to a blue floral print quarter-square triangle. Press. Sew the units together and press. Make four.

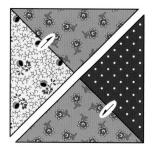
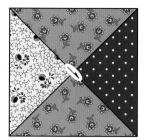

Make 4.

7. Arrange the Schoolhouse blocks with the Hourglass blocks into three rows, as shown. Sew the blocks into rows and press. Sew the rows together and press the seams toward the middle row.

8. Sew the 2¼" x 12½" strips of blue floral print to the top and bottom of the quilt top. Press the seams toward the border. Add the 2¼" x 16" strips of blue floral print to the sides of the quilt top, pressing seams toward the border.

Finishing the Quilt

1. Layer the quilt top, batting and backing, and baste the layers together as shown in "Putting the Quilt Together" on page 75.

2. Quilt in the ditch around each block and window rectangle.

3. Attach the light print binding to the quilt, referring to "Single-Fold Binding" on page 76.

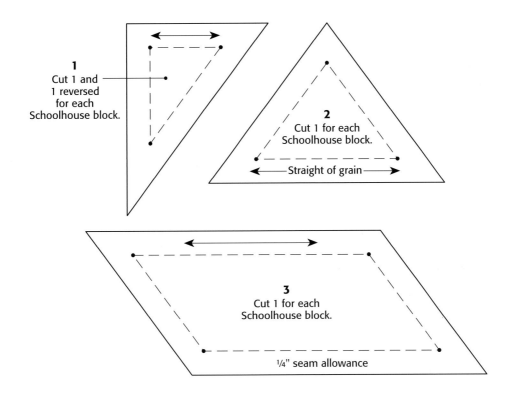

1
Cut 1 and 1 reversed for each Schoolhouse block.

2
Cut 1 for each Schoolhouse block.
← Straight of grain →

3
Cut 1 for each Schoolhouse block.

¼" seam allowance

The sampler has a long tradition in American needlework. Young schoolgirls may have practiced sewing and quilting simple blocks until they were more proficient at the craft in the same way they worked their needlepoint samplers.

Materials

Yardages are based on 42"-wide, 100%-cotton fabrics.

- ✦ 1 yard *total* of assorted light, medium, and dark print scraps in shades of white, pink, blue, brown, and tan for blocks
- ✦ ¼ yard of pink plaid for border
- ✦ ¼ yard of light blue print for binding
- ✦ ⅝ yard of fabric for backing
- ✦ 21" x 25" piece of cotton batting

Cutting for Border and Binding

From the pink plaid, cut:

- ✦ 2 strips, 3" x 42", crosscut into 2 pieces, 3" x 12½", and 2 pieces, 3" x 21½"

From the light blue print for binding, cut:

- ✦ 3 strips, 1½" x 42"

Making the Blocks

To simplify assembly, cutting and piecing directions for each block are given separately. Try to use a different combination of light, medium, and dark scraps in each block.

CROSSES AND LOSSES BLOCK

From a pink scrap, cut:

- ✦ 1 square, 2⅞" x 2⅞"

From a white scrap, cut:

- ✦ 1 square, 2⅞" x 2⅞"
- ✦ 2 squares, 1⅞" x 1⅞"
- ✦ 4 squares, 1½" x 1½"

From a brown scrap, cut:

- ✦ 2 squares, 1⅞" x 1⅞"

1. Draw a diagonal line from corner to corner on the wrong side of each 1⅞" white square. Layer a marked square on each 1⅞" brown square, right sides together. Stitch ¼" from the line on both sides. Cut on the drawn line. Press. Make four half-square-triangle units.

Make 4.

2. Draw a diagonal line on the wrong side of the 2⅞" white square. Layer the marked square on the 2⅞" pink square, right sides together. Stitch ¼" from the line on both sides. Cut on the drawn line to make two half-square-triangle units. Press.

Make 2.

3. Pair one unit from step 1 together with a 1½" white square, as shown. Press. Make four.

Make 4.

4. Using the units from steps 2 and 3, assemble the Crosses and Losses block as shown.

SQUARE IN A SQUARE BLOCK

From a blue scrap, cut:

+ 1 square, 2½" x 2½"
+ 2 squares, 2⅞" x 2⅞"; cut each square in half diagonally once

From a pink scrap, cut:

+ 1 square, 3¼" x 3¼"; cut in half diagonally twice

1. Sew the pink triangles to the sides of the 2½" blue square. Press.

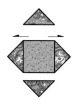

2. Sew the blue triangles to the sides of the unit from step 1. Press.

CHECKERBOARD BLOCK

From a blue scrap, cut:

+ 6 squares, 1½" x 1½"

From a white scrap, cut:

+ 6 squares, 1½" x 1½"

From a brown scrap, cut:

+ 1 square, 2½" x 2½"

1. Sew each 1½" blue square to a 1½" white square. Make six units. Press four toward the dark fabric and two toward the light fabric.

Make 6.

2. Sew a step 1 unit pressed toward the dark fabric to opposite sides of the 2½" brown square. Press toward the center square.

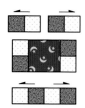

3. Sew the remaining units together as shown to make the Checkerboard block.

RECTANGULAR FOUR PATCH BLOCK

From a medium blue scrap, cut:

+ 4 rectangles, 1½" x 2½"

From a contrasting blue scrap, cut:

+ 4 rectangles, 1½" x 2½"

1. Stitch one 1½" x 2½" blue rectangle to a contrasting 1½" x 2½" blue rectangle. Press. Make four.

Make 4.

2. Sew the four units together to make the rectangular Four Patch block as shown. Press.

Flying Geese Block

From a light pink scrap, cut:

✦ 16 squares, 1½" x 1½"

From a medium pink scrap, cut:

✦ 8 rectangles, 1½" x 2½"

1. Draw a diagonal line from corner to corner on the wrong side of each 1½" light pink square.

2. Layer a marked square on one end of a 1½" x 2½" medium pink rectangle, right sides together, as shown. Sew on the line and trim to a ¼" seam allowance. Press the triangle toward the corner. Place another marked square on the opposite end of the medium pink rectangle, right sides together, making sure the diagonal line is oriented in the opposite direction from the first piece. Stitch on the drawn line. Trim to a ¼" seam allowance and press the triangle toward the corner. Make eight flying-geese units.

Make 8.

3. Sew the units together as shown to make the Flying Geese block.

Pinwheel Block

From a light blue scrap, cut:

✦ 2 squares, 2⅞" x 2⅞"

From a brown scrap, cut:

✦ 2 squares, 2⅞" x 2⅞"

1. Draw a diagonal line from corner to corner on the wrong side of each 2⅞" light blue square. Layer a marked square on each 2⅞" brown square, right sides together. Stitch ¼" from the drawn line on both sides. Cut on the drawn line. Press toward the brown fabric. Make four half-square-triangle units.

Make 4.

2. Sew the units together as shown to make a Pinwheel block. Press.

Homeward Bound Block

From a tan scrap, cut:

✦ 1 square, 2⅞" x 2⅞"

From a pink scrap, cut:

✦ 1 square, 2⅞" x 2⅞"

From a brown scrap, cut:

✦ 2 squares, 2½" x 2½"

1. Draw a diagonal line on the wrong side of the 2⅞" tan square. Layer the marked square on top of the 2⅞" pink square. Stitch ¼" from the line on both sides. Cut on the drawn line to make two half-square-triangle units. Press toward the darker fabric.

Make 2.

2. Sew each unit from step 1 to a 2½" brown square and sew the units together to make the Home-ward Bound block.

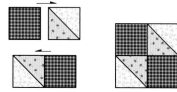

SAWTOOTH STAR BLOCK

From a brown scrap, cut:
+ 8 squares, 1½" x 1½"

From a light blue scrap, cut:
+ 4 rectangles, 1½" x 2½"
+ 4 squares, 1½" x 1½"

From a medium blue scrap, cut:
+ 1 square, 2½" x 2½"

1. Draw a diagonal line from corner to corner on the wrong side of each 1½" brown square.

2. Layer a marked square on one end of a 1½" x 2½" light blue rectangle, right sides together, as shown. Sew on the line and trim to a ¼" seam allowance. Press the triangle toward the corner. Place another marked square on the other end of the rectangle, right sides together, making sure the diagonal line is oriented in the opposite direction from the first piece. Stitch on the drawn line. Trim to a ¼" seam allowance and press the triangle toward the corner. Make four flying-geese units.

Make 4.

3. Sew a 1½" light blue square to each end of two of the flying-geese units and press the seams toward the squares. Sew the two remaining flying-geese units to each side of the 2½" medium blue square,

and press the seams toward the square. Sew the rows together as shown and press the seams to-ward the center row to make the Sawtooth Star block.

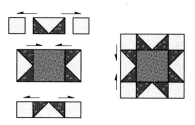

DOUBLE FOUR PATCH BLOCK

From a white scrap, cut:
+ 4 squares, 1½" x 1½"

From a dark pink scrap, cut:
+ 4 squares, 1½" x 1½"

From a contrasting medium scrap, cut:
+ 2 squares, 2½" x 2½"

1. Sew a 1½" dark pink square to a 1½" white square. Press toward the dark pink fabric. Make four.

Make 4.

2. Sew two units from step 1 together to make a four-patch unit. Press. Make two.

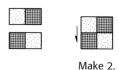

Make 2.

3. Sew the four-patch units together with the 2½" medium squares to make the Double Four Patch block.

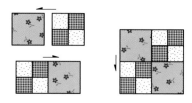

SOUTHERN BELLE BLOCK

From a medium tan scrap, cut:
+ 1 square, 3¼" x 3¼"; cut in half diagonally twice

From a blue scrap, cut:
+ 1 square, 3¼" x 3¼"; cut in half diagonally twice

From a light tan scrap, cut:
+ 1 square, 2⅞" x 2⅞"; cut in half diagonally once

From a pink scrap, cut:
+ 1 square, 2⅞" x 2⅞"; cut in half diagonally once

1. Sew a medium tan quarter-square triangle to a blue quarter-square triangle, right sides together, as shown. Press. Make four.

Make 4.

2. Sew two of the units from step 1 together with a pink half-square triangle. Press. Sew the remaining units from step 1 to the light tan half-square triangles. Press. Make two.

Make 2 of each.

3. Sew the units together as shown to make the Southern Belle block.

FRAMED FOUR PATCH BLOCK

From a dark blue scrap, cut:
+ 2 squares, 1½" x 1½"

From a dark pink scrap, cut:
+ 2 squares, 1½" x 1½"

From a medium blue scrap, cut:
+ 4 squares, 1½" x 1½"

From a tan scrap, cut:
+ 4 rectangles, 1½" x 2½"

1. Sew a 1½" dark blue square to a 1½" pink square. Press toward the dark pink fabric. Make two. Assemble into a four-patch unit as shown.

Make 2.

2. Sew a 1½" medium blue square to the short ends of two of the 1½" x 2½" tan rectangles. Press toward the blue fabric.

Make 2.

3. Sew the two remaining 1½" x 2½" tan rectangles to the sides of the four-patch unit. Add the units from step 2 to complete the Framed Four Patch block.

Sixteen Patch Block

From a variety of light and dark scraps, cut:

✦ 16 squares, 1½" x 1½"

1. Sew the squares together into groups of four. Make four.

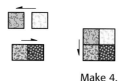

Make 4.

2. Assemble the four-patch units into a Sixteen Patch block as shown.

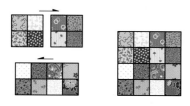

Assembling the Quilt Top

1. Arrange the blocks into four rows of three blocks each, referring to the diagram at right for placement. Sew the blocks into rows, pressing the seams in the opposite direction from row to row.

2. Sew the 3" x 12½" pink plaid strips to the top and bottom of the quilt top. Press toward the border. Add the 3" x 21½" pink plaid strips to the sides of the quilt top. Press toward the border.

Finishing the Quilt

1. Layer the quilt top, batting, and backing, and baste the layers together as shown in "Putting the Quilt Together" on page 75.

2. Quilt as desired in each block and in the borders.

3. Attach the blue binding to the quilt, referring to "Single-Fold Binding" on page 76.

QUILTMAKING BASICS

QUILTING IN AMERICA has changed significantly since the 1800s. Women at that time made use of simple, practical designs because of the necessity of making bedding as fast as they were able, in what little time they had. Many of the blocks that were named for the pioneers' daily experiences were handed down from that period and are still used by quilters today. Pioneer women pieced their lives into their quilts, and the quilting patterns they created have stood the test of time, becoming firmly established in American quilt-making traditions today.

Most of the quilts in this book use just a few basic blocks or units that combine squares or triangles, such as the Four Patch, Nine Patch, Triangle Square, Flying Geese, and Hourglass. To make the quilts you will need a very basic sewing machine.

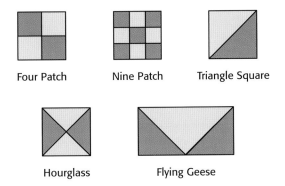

Four Patch   Nine Patch   Triangle Square

Hourglass   Flying Geese

Use a ¼" seam allowance and try to be accurate. If your machine doesn't have a ¼" foot, place a strip of masking tape on the throat plate exactly ¼" from the needle and use it as a guide when you sew.

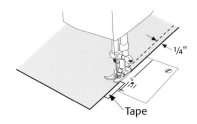

¼"

Tape

Doll quilts with a naive, childlike quality have an appeal that draws us to them. This look can be achieved by relaxing and having fun while making your quilt instead of fussing too much about perfect seams or tiny stitches. A little irregularity in the quilt adds a simple charm that reminds us of antique quilts made long ago.

Tools

Even the smallest projects require a few basic tools.

Rotary cutter: A medium-sized cutter (45 mm) will enable you to cut strips and trim small pieces.

Ruler: Use a clear plastic ruler that is at least 4" x 12", designed for use with a rotary cutter. The measurements should be clearly marked. A 6" square ruler also comes in handy.

Rotary-cutting mat: Use this gridded surface for cutting fabric. The 18" x 24" size is a good choice.

Pins: Use sharp pins to hold your pieces while sewing.

Thread: Always use 100%-cotton thread for your piecing, and use quilting thread, which is coated, for hand quilting.

Needles: Use 80/12 sewing machine needles for machine piecing. Change your needle after every major project to be sure your needle is always sharp. You will need basic hand sewing needles for turning bindings and needles called Betweens for hand quilting.

Seam ripper: Expect to make some mistakes, but don't worry too much about them. If you do make a serious mistake, a seam ripper helps you take the stitches out to correct it.

Iron and pressing surface: Any iron with a cotton setting will work for pressing your quilt pieces. You will need a flat surface for pressing, such as an ironing board or pressing mat.

Doll quilts from the past relied heavily on scraps, because that was what was available. Many of the quilts in this book were made with scraps from my scrap basket, just as the pioneers utilized what they had left over or were able to salvage from worn clothing. ✑

Rotary Cutting

Accurate cutting is an important part of making any quilt, large or small. If your pieces are not cut properly, the piecing may be difficult and the quilt measurements will be off. Cutting is also important for conserving your fabric, although these small quilts use a variety of scraps, and you can substitute a similar fabric if needed to "make do." There should be adequate fabrics based on yardage amounts given in the pattern directions.

While strip piecing and cutting doesn't work too well with scrap quilts, as no two blocks are usually the same, you *can* layer your different fabrics and cut multiple fabrics at the same time.

Pressing

Always press each seam after sewing. Press the seams to one side, toward the darker fabric if possible. To join together pieces, blocks, or rows of blocks, press the seam allowances in opposite directions to make matching the seams easier. Pressing in this way will allow seams to line up more easily and the blocks will fit together nicely.

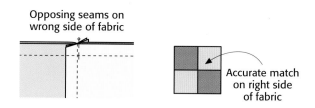

Borders

Small quilts can always be finished with a simple binding instead of a border, but a border can enhance the quilt if it is chosen well. I rarely choose border fabric until after the center of the quilt top is completed. Many times I will carry the top around with me on my travels to quilt shops until I find just the right print that complements the design. Fabrics can definitely speak to us and if you "audition" a fabric for a border by placing it next to the finished quilt top, pay attention to whether it feels right. Is the fabric so bright or busy that it detracts from the quilt? The border should

A Note to Beginning Quilters

To successfully make small quilts that are proportioned well and to keep your small blocks the same size, it is important to slow down when you are sewing and measure each block before you piece it with another. Because small quilts are often so simple to make and quick to finish, we are tempted to hurry to get them done and move on to the next one. Many new quilters make mistakes when they rush. If your sewing machine has a mechanism to adjust the sewing speed, don't set it too fast. You'll find that you make fewer mistakes, and you won't need to stop as often to rip out seams and resew them.

frame the quilt, not take over. If your top is particularly busy with many scrappy pieces, you may not want to choose a large print. Busy borders work best when the rest of the quilt has a subdued tone and contains fewer contrasting pieces.

It is always important to measure the sewn quilt top before cutting the border strips. Measure from the center in both directions and cut the borders accordingly.

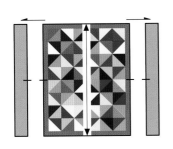 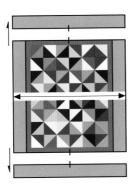

Putting the Quilt Together

Square up the four corners of your quilt top using a square ruler. Trim the four sides, if necessary, by lining up your long ruler from one corner to the opposite corner and trimming off any excess fabric.

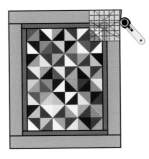 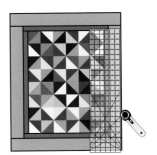

Use a thin, low-loft cotton batting for the soft, flat look seen in many antique quilts. Cut the batting and backing at least 3" larger in length and width than the quilt top. Lay the backing on a smooth, clean surface. Keeping it taut but not stretched, secure the backing to the surface with masking tape. Layer the batting and quilt top over the backing. Baste or pin the layers together.

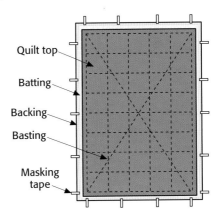

Quilt top
Batting
Backing
Basting
Masking tape

Quilting

Quilting by hand is a luxury that many women today cannot afford unless they make small quilts. All the quilts in this book were quilted by hand, using simple quilting designs for a primitive look. You may prefer to quilt them by machine using similar quilting patterns. I find that quilting by hand is one of the simplest and most relaxing of needlework skills and requires just a little bit of practice.

Cut an 18" length of neutral-colored quilting thread. You can also use a thread that matches the fabrics on the quilt top, or even a contrasting thread if you want your stitches to stand out. Try to keep your stitches even, but remember—they don't have to be tiny and perfect to get that childlike handmade look!

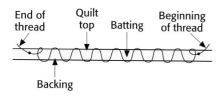

Single-Fold Binding

I like to use a single-fold binding on these small quilts because it adds less bulk, and a double-fold binding is not needed for durability.

1. Measure around the quilt, and add 10" extra for mitering corners and joining strips. This can be cut off later. Cut enough 1½"-wide strips across the width of the binding fabric to achieve the total length necessary. Join the strips using a diagonal seam.

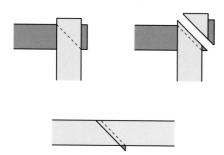

2. Using your ruler and rotary cutter, make sure the corners form accurate right angles, and straighten the edges of the quilt if needed. Trim away the excess batting and backing.

3. Cut one end of the binding on the diagonal, fold over ¼", and press, wrong sides together. Position the binding along one side of the quilt, right sides together and with raw edges aligned.

4. Stitch the binding to the quilt top, starting at the center of one side and using a ¼" seam allowance. Sew through all three layers. Stop ¼" from the first corner and backstitch.

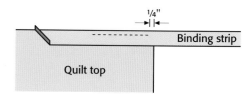

5. Remove the quilt from the machine. Turn the quilt and fold the binding straight up, making a 45° angle. Fold the binding back down, aligning it with the edge of the next side. Continue sewing the remaining sides in this way. When you come to the place you started, stitch over the end you folded at the beginning and trim the excess.

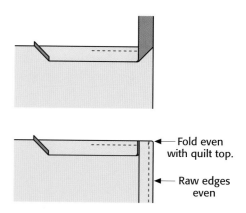

6. Turn the binding over to the back of the quilt. Turn the raw edge under ¼" and slip-stitch it to the back of the quilt using matching thread. Miter each of the corners as shown.

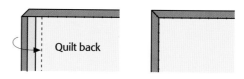

BIBLIOGRAPHY

Fry, Gladys-Marie. *Stitched from the Soul: Slave Quilts from the Antebellum South.* New York: Dutton Studio Books, 1990.

Hine, Darlene Clark, and Kathleen Thompson. *A Shining Thread of Hope: The History of Black Women in America.* New York: Broadway Books, 1998.

Holmes, Kenneth. *Covered Wagon Women: Diaries & Letters from the Western Trails, 1840–1849.* Lincoln, NE: University of Nebraska Press, 1995.

_____. *Covered Wagon Women: Diaries & Letters from the Western Trails, 1852.* Lincoln, NE: University of Nebraska Press, 1997.

_____. *Covered Wagon Women: Diaries & Letters from the Western Trails, 1862–1865.* Lincoln, NE: University of Nebraska Press, 1995.

Holt, Marilyn Irvin. *Children of the Western Plains.* Chicago: Ivan R. Dee, 2003.

Johnson, Anne. *America's Quilting History.* www.womenfolk.com/historyofquilts. 2006.

Jones, Mary Ellen. *Daily Life on the 19th-Century American Frontier.* Westport, CT: Greenwood Press, 1998.

Kimball, Violet T. *Stories of Young Pioneers.* Missoula, MT: Mountain Press Publishing Co., 2000.

Kiracofe, Roderick. *The American Quilt: A History of Cloth and Comfort 1750–1950.* New York: Clarkson Potter, 1993.

Kolter, Jane Bentley. *Forget Me Not: A Gallery of Friendship and Album Quilts.* Pittstown, NJ: Main Street Press, 1985.

Kort, Ellen. *Wisconsin Quilts: Stories in the Stitches.* Charlottesville, VA: Howell Press, 2001.

Leon, Eli. *Who'd a Thought It: Improvisation in African-American Quiltmaking.* San Francisco, CA: San Francisco Craft and Folk Art Museum, 1988.

Lipsett, Linda Otto. *Remember Me: Women and Their Friendship Quilts.* Lincolnwood, IL: The Quilt Digest Press, 1985.

Lucetti, Cathy. *Children of the West: Family Life on the Frontier.* New York: W. W. Norton & Co., 2001.

Madsen, Susan Arrington. *I Walked to Zion: True Stories of Young Pioneers on the Mormon Trail.* Salt Lake City, UT: Deseret Book Company, 1994.

Nugent, Walter. *Into the West: The Story of Its People.* New York: Alfred A. Knopf, 1999.

O'Brien, Mary Barmeyer. *Toward the Setting Sun: Pioneer Girls Traveling the Overland Trails.* Helena, MT: Falcon Publishing, Inc., 2000.

Peavy, Linda, and Ursula Smith. *Frontier Children.* Norman, OK: University of Oklahoma Press, 1999.

_____. *Pioneer Women: The Lives of Women on the Frontier.* New York: Smithmark Publishers, 1996.

Schlissel, Lillian. *Women's Diaries of the Westward Journey.* New York: Schocken Books, 1982.

Shaw, Robert. *America's Traditional Crafts.* New York: Hugh Lauter Levin Associates, Inc., 1983.

_____. *Quilts: A Living Tradition.* New York: Hugh Lauter Levin Associates, Inc., 1995.

Steffof, Rebecca. *Children of the Westward Trail.* Brookfield, CT: Millbrook Press, 1996.

_____. *The Oregon Trail in American History.* Springfield, NJ: Enslow Publishers Inc., 1997.

Wadsworth, Ginger. *Words West: Voices of Young Pioneers.* New York: Clarion Books, 2003.

Werner, Emmy E. *Pioneer Children on the Journey West.* Boulder, CO: Westview Press, Inc., 1995.

Wilder, Laura Ingalls. *Little House in the Big Woods.* New York: Harper & Row, 1953.

_____. *These Happy Golden Years.* New York: Harper & Row, 1943.

Wulfert, Kimberly. *New Pathways into Quilt History.* www.antiquequiltdating.com, 2006.

Early Transportation In The Dakotas.

ABOUT THE AUTHOR

KATHLEEN TRACY, an editor in the publishing industry for over twenty years, began making small quilts in 2000. She soon turned her hobby into a profession with her pattern and kit business, Country Lane Quilts (www.countrylanequilts.com). Kathleen holds a particular interest in antique quilts and the women who made them, and she hopes that her books inspire others to learn more about America's quilting heritage. She lectures to quilt guilds and teaches workshops on small quilts and their historical significance. Kathleen's first book, *American Doll Quilts,* published in 2004, was a Martingale & Company bestseller. She lives in Deerfield, Illinois, with her husband, two children, and their wheaten terrier.

New and Bestselling Titles from

Martingale®
& C O M P A N Y

America's Best-Loved Craft & Hobby Books®
America's Best-Loved Knitting Books®

That Patchwork Place®

America's Best-Loved Quilt Books®

NEW RELEASES
Adoration Quilts
Better by the Dozen
Blessed Home Quilt, The
Hooked on Wool
It's a Wrap
Let's Quilt!
Origami Quilts
Over Easy
Primitive Gatherings
Quilt Revival
Sew One and You're Done
Scraps of Time
Simple Chenille Quilts
Simple Traditions
Simply Primitive
Surprisingly Simple Quilts
Two-Block Theme Quilts
Wheel of Mystery Quilts

APPLIQUÉ
Appliqué Takes Wing
Easy Appliqué Samplers
Garden Party
Raise the Roof
Stitch and Split Appliqué
Tea in the Garden

LEARNING TO QUILT
Happy Endings, Revised Edition
Loving Stitches, Revised Edition
Magic of Quiltmaking, The
Quilter's Quick Reference Guide, The
Your First Quilt Book (or it should be!)

PAPER PIECING
40 Bright and Bold Paper-Pieced Blocks
50 Fabulous Paper-Pieced Stars
300 Paper-Pieced Quilt Blocks
Easy Machine Paper Piecing
Quilt Block Bonanza
Quilter's Ark, A
Show Me How to Paper Piece

PIECING
40 Fabulous Quick-Cut Quilts
101 Fabulous Rotary-Cut Quilts
365 Quilt Blocks a Year: Perpetual
    Calendar
1000 Great Quilt Blocks
Big 'n Easy
Clever Quilts Encore
Once More around the Block
Stack a New Deck

QUILTS FOR BABIES & CHILDREN
American Doll Quilts
Even More Quilts for Baby
More Quilts for Baby
Quilts for Baby
Sweet and Simple Baby Quilts

SCRAP QUILTS
More Nickel Quilts
Nickel Quilts
Save the Scraps
Successful Scrap Quilts
    from Simple Rectangles
Treasury of Scrap Quilts, A

TOPICS IN QUILTMAKING
Alphabet Soup
Cottage-Style Quilts
Creating Your Perfect Quilting Space
Focus on Florals
Follow the Dots . . . to Dazzling Quilts
More Biblical Quilt Blocks
Scatter Garden Quilts
Sensational Sashiko
Warm Up to Wool

CRAFTS
Bag Boutique
Purely Primitive
Scrapbooking Off the Page…and on the
    Wall
Stamp in Color
Vintage Workshop, The: Gifts for All
    Occasions

KNITTING & CROCHET
200 Knitted Blocks
365 Knitting Stitches a Year: Perpetual
    Calendar
Crochet from the Heart
First Crochet
First Knits
Fun and Funky Crochet
Handknit Style
Knits from the Heart
Little Box of Knitted Ponchos and Wraps,
    The
Little Box of Knitted Throws, The
Little Box of Crocheted Hats and Scarves,
    The
Little Box of Scarves, The
Little Box of Scarves II, The
Little Box of Sweaters, The
Pursenalities
Sensational Knitted Socks

Our books are available at bookstores and your favorite craft,
fabric, and yarn retailers. If you don't see the title
you're looking for, visit us at
www.martingale-pub.com
or contact us at:

1-800-426-3126

International: 1-425-483-3313 **Fax:** 1-425-486-7596
Email: info@martingale-pub.com

05/06